KU-745-718

Cuisine Courante

Cuisine Courante

BRUNO LOUBET

Text in association with Norma MacMillan

Amitiés Gourmands
Bruno

PAVILION

First published in Great Britain in 1991 by
PAVILION BOOKS LIMITED
196 Shaftesbury Avenue, London WC2H 8JL

Text copyright © Bruno Loubet 1991
Text in association with Norma MacMillan
Photographs copyright © Sue Atkinson 1991

Designed by Elizabeth Ayer

All rights reserved. No part of this publication
may be reproduced, stored in a retrieval system, or
transmitted, in any form or by any means, electronic,
mechanical, photocopying, recording or otherwise,
without the prior permission of the copyright holder.

A CIP catalogue record for this book is
available from the British Library

ISBN 1 85145 652 X

10 9 8 7 6 5 4 3 2 1

Typeset by DP Photosetting, Aylesbury, Bucks
Printed and bound in Italy
by Graphicom

CONTENTS

INTRODUCTION

AS far back as I can remember, I wanted to be a chef. I was always interested in food as a child, and ate everything. I was very fat! We had a large vegetable garden at home and some poultry, and it was my job to look after these. I used to spend at least two hours every day working in the garden and with the poultry, and I learned a lot from it. When the lovely vegetables and poultry arrived on our table, 'you can't imagine how proud I was. I think this is one of the major reasons why I have so much respect for food.

I was born and brought up in Libourne, which is a small town between St Emilion and Pomerol in the southwest of France – what we call 'Le Grand Sud'ouest'. My father's family were farmers in the area, and I have many aunts, uncles and cousins still living there (in fact, all but one of my brothers and four sisters have stayed in Bordeaux). My father had to work hard to keep all of us, and so that we could have a month's holiday every summer, he did two jobs at the same time – one for the French railway and the other for a rich wine-maker, working in the vineyards and the gardens. We children, too, worked in the vineyards. As a boy of 7, I started picking grapes and carrying baskets for 1 franc a day.

During the *vendange*, when the grapes were picked, the wine-maker liked to impress his workers with how rich and generous he was, so he put on a great feast and we all ate very well. My family also had a huge feast every year at my grandparents' farm, when the pigs were killed at the beginning of winter. My father would make the black pudding (which was then cooked in a soup we called *zimbura*), my uncles the hams, and my mother and aunts the *farces* for pâtés and the andouillettes. And my grandmother would run the whole show like a general. When we sat down to eat, there could be 50 or more of us at the long tables under the lime trees.

At other times of the year, when the family finances weren't too good, I can remember going to bed and dreaming about roast poultry, meat stew and charcuterie appearing with the wave of a magic wand. Looking back today, I am sure that this helped me to appreciate and recognise the flavours of simple, honest cooking.

School was not my cup of tea, and seeing my parents working so hard, I decided to support myself. So making what seemed an obvious choice, I went to the catering school in Bordeaux at age 14. To pay all my expenses, I worked every weekend and holiday in a restaurant as a waiter.

After 3 years, I passed my diploma, and started my first job in the kitchen of a small restaurant in the southwest. It was then that I bought a book that had a great effect on me. It was *Cuisine Minceur* by Michel Guérard. I read this book and read it again, asking myself why I had just spent 3 years in catering school learning about soft-boiled eggs on spinach with Béchamel sauce! I quickly understood that cooking needs not only energy and understanding, but a personal touch as well, that comes from the heart, and opens the doors to freedom. A further book by Michael Guérard, *Cuisine Gourmande*, strengthened my views on 'cooking as you feel'.

I moved to Brussels, to work as *chef-saucier* at the Hyatt-Regency Hotel, and then to Paris to the Michelin-starred Le Copenhague. My year there still inspires some Scandinavian touches in my cooking today, such as hot smoked salmon.

Then I was called up to do my national service, in the Navy. I was head chef for the Admiral's table. For many, national service was a waste of time, but I learnt a lot from producing food for large and important receptions as well as the many private receptions hosted by the senior officers.

After I was discharged, I applied for a job with various Michelin-starred restaurants. My only favourable answer came from La Tante Claire in London, and so in 1982 I began work there. Unfortunately, it was only a brief stay, but my sojourn at Gastronome One in Fulham was longer and much happier, and in 1985, The Good Food Guide voted me the 'Young Chef of the Year'!

The next year, I met Raymond Blanc at his superb Manoir aux Quat'Saisons. We had a long talk about our passions for food and cooking and, after about 2 hours, he asked me if I would like to work for him at Le Manoir. It was such a shock that I requested 2 weeks to think about it.

After deliberating, I accepted his offer. A year in the kitchen at Le Manoir proved to me that Raymond Blanc is one of the rare chefs to be honest with himself, with such a passion about his work as well as respect and conviviality for his customers. If something is not 100 percent up to his standard, it will be thrown in the bin and all will be started again. He will not compromise.

In September 1986, Raymond entrusted me with the job of head chef/manager of his restaurant Le Petit Blanc in Oxford where, over the course of 2 happy and successful years, I started to develop my own style of cooking, reworking classic dishes – particularly those from my native Bordeaux – to make them more modern but still keeping things simple and full of intense flavours. Raymond Blanc challenged me to think twice and so avoid the mistake of routine.

I believe that you must bring something to a dish to enhance the flavour, but if your approach is too complicated you will disguise its intrinsic qualities. I try to use the least number of ingredients because if food is too clever and sophisticated, the palate is confused.

My cooking is very honest – some may call it characterful, others may say it is hearty and earthy. Many chefs work according to the fashions and for the celebrities, never cooking the dishes they would like to eat themselves. I cook what I like, not what is regarded as fashionable.

Since March 1989, I have been Chef de Cuisine at the Four Seasons Restaurant at the Inn on the Park Hotel in London, and am very proud to have now achieved my first Michelin star. I feel I have been very lucky to have reached this stage.

Chefs work very hard – on a normal day, it's 9am to 3.30pm, then 6.30pm to midnight, and if we have a lot of people, or a banquet, or a new menu, it can run to 18 hours or so. The atmosphere in some restaurant kitchens can be tense and angry, under such pressure, but I believe strongly that the chefs who work for me, my *brigade*, should be praised for their achievements, as well as criticised for their mistakes. I take care not to lose my temper because I think that a cook who is happy will produce work three times as good as one who is unhappy. I think this is why so many chefs stay in my kitchen – which is a demanding one – for 2 years or more.

You pay a high price to succeed in this profession – like an athlete running in the Olympics, you have to give everything, and still this does not always win you a place on the podium.

I personally cannot see myself doing anything else. Cooking and my wife are my two best friends, and I hope I will keep them for life.

A LESSON IN TASTE
In the summer of 1984, my wife's grandparents invited us to have dinner with them at Alain Chapel's restaurant at Mionnay, near Lyon. The meal, service and atmosphere were a feast.

My first course had the most exciting flavours I had ever tasted: *Mille feuilles de crêtes et rognons de coq, écrevisses pattes rouges aux mousserons et jus de cerfeuil.* This dish was such a revelation to me that today, nearly seven years later, I can still remember every detail of its conception and flavours.

This dish had such an impact on my palate and my professional life that I would choose it as my last supper. And if God does not let me into Paradise, it would not matter so much now that I have had a taste of Paradise in this world.

BRUNO LOUBET,
1990

INGREDIENTS AND TECHNIQUES

CUISINE NOUVELLE uses expensive ingredients, in small quantities, but I believe a good chef or cook should be able to take any produce and make it interesting. At The Four Seasons, I have the most expensive products available from all over the world; what I like to do is to mix them with what could be called 'poor' ingredients. In fact, I prefer to use cheaper cuts of meat in my cooking – knuckle or shank of veal or neck fillet of lamb – rather than those considered to be the best.

The recipes in this book have been simplified so that they can be made at home – without a brigade of chefs to help. Most of the ingredients are widely available in supermarkets. Where something may be more difficult to find, I've tried to suggest an alternative. I also give here some notes about the ingredients I like and use most – some of which may be a little unfamiliar to you.

AROMATICS AND SEASONINGS
Maldon sea salt: I use this all the time, mainly for fish dishes, but also for preserved meats such as *confit* or ham. It has a beautiful texture and mild, salty flavour. I rarely add Maldon sea salt to a dish while it is cooking (ordinary table salt is fine for this if you need to add salt), but instead sprinkle it over the food just before serving so its rough, crunchy texture can be appreciated.

Green peppercorns: These are unripe peppercorns (the black are fully ripe). They have a subtle and interesting flavour that is especially good in a game sauce, used in small quantity. I prefer the dried peppercorns to those bottled in brine.

Herbs: I am crazy about herbs in my cooking – and they must be fresh because of their texture and flavour. I use fresh herbs in nearly every dish – one, two or three herbs, but never more or the flavours become confusing. Herbs are for me a symbol of freshness and freedom.

Bouquet garni: This bouquet or small bunch of herbs usually contains parsley, thyme and bay leaves, but you can add other aromatic ingredients depending on the recipe. For example, a bouquet garni for white meat could comprise parsley, bay leaf, tarragon, celery and onion studded with cloves; for red meat, parsley, thyme, bay leaf and tarragon; for game, thyme, bay leaf, celeriac (celery root) or celery leaves, juniper berries, orange zest and onion studded with cloves. Just remember that the bouquet garni should complement the flavours in a dish, not dominate them. I always prepare a bouquet garni with whole fresh herbs and spices, wrapped in a small muslin or cheesecloth bag. Just before adding the bouquet garni to the cooking pot, I chop it a few times with the blunt edge of a knife, to bruise the herbs and release their flavoured oils.

Parsley: In most cases, I prefer to use flat-leaf rather than curly parsley. This is because it has a stronger flavour.

Garlic: This is one of the biggest ambassadors of French cuisine – it appears in so many dishes, and always gives a sunny flavour. For many recipes, I just crush the garlic clove with the side of a heavy knife blade before adding it – this allows all the garlic 'essence' to be taken into the preparation without it being overpowering (the more garlic is mashed or chopped, the stronger its flavour will be).

Lemon grass: The thick stalks or sticks of this grass from Southeast Asia have a sweet lemon flavour with a touch of ginger. You can buy fresh lemon grass in many supermarkets, or look for it in oriental shops.

Cardamom: This pod, containing lots of tiny black seeds, is the fruit of a plant of the ginger family, native to India. It is one of my favourite spices, with a very distinct and deep flavour. If the whole pod is added to a dish, I usually first crush it lightly with the side of a knife.

Coriander seeds: To fully appreciate the perfume and flavour of this spice, I recommend that you lightly fry the seeds in a dry frying pan just until they smell aromatic, then lightly crush or add whole to the dish. Do the same for juniper berries and other similar whole spices.

Cumin: The dried fruit of a plant related to parsley, cumin comes as whole seeds or ground. It has a slightly hot, bitter taste, which I love in a sauce for fish or in a rice preparation.

Nutmeg: Always use nutmeg freshly grated – the already ground spice has little flavour or pungency compared to fresh. I like nutmeg in mashed potatoes and white sauce, but prefer to use mace (which is the thin covering on the nutmeg kernel) in a sauce for fish.

Saffron: The dried stigmas of a crocus native to Greece, saffron is the most expensive spice in the world (I know a store in London that keeps £80,000 worth of saffron in just a few boxes). A very good thing, then, that you need only a very small quantity to enhance the flavour and colour of a sauce or other preparation!

Star anise: These beautiful star-shaped pods are the dried fruit of an evergreen tree native to China. They have a strong aniseed flavour. I enjoy using oriental spices like star anise – although I am not in favour of change just for the sake of it, it is interesting to try ingredients that are outside the traditions of French cuisine.

Turmeric: This is sometimes used to colour food yellow in place of saffron, although it doesn't have the delicate flavour of that more expensive spice. Turmeric is much used in Indian cookery – it is a usual component of curry powder. I like to use it in lamb dishes.

Vanilla: I use vanilla pods (vanilla beans) in creams, and vanilla sugar in baking. The vanilla essence (vanilla extract) you can buy in bottles does not give the same rich vanilla flavour (if you want to use vanilla essence, for maximum flavour add it to your cream once it has cooled). It's easy to make your own vanilla sugar: split open 4 vanilla pods lengthways so the tiny black seeds are exposed, place the pods in a jar and cover with 500 g/ 1 lb 2 oz/2½ cups of caster or granulated sugar. Leave for at least a week before using.

VINEGARS, MUSTARDS AND SAUCES

Vinegars: I use wine vinegar – both red and white – a lot. The darker red wine vinegars are made from better quality wine than those vinegars that are light and clear so they have a richer flavour. A combination of *vin piqué* (sour wine – see page 79) and red wine vinegar is especially good in a cooked sauce.

I prefer to make herb vinegars rather than buy them – simply boil white wine vinegar, add fresh herbs such as tarragon and leave to infuse. And I rarely use fruit vinegars, which I think are one of the unnecessary things that *cuisine nouvelle* chefs have introduced. A fruit vinegar doesn't bring very much flavour to food – for a fruity flavour, I prefer to add mashed fresh berries to a cooking liquid and then to reduce it and sieve it to a sauce.

Balsamic vinegar has a wonderful flavour. I use it cold in dressing but rarely in a hot preparation – it's a shame to put it into a hot sauce because it's expensive and, like a good olive oil, it will lose 80 percent of its flavour when heated.

The clear, white Chinese or Japanese rice vinegar is light in flavour and slightly sweet. If you cannot find it, you can substitute cider vinegar with a pinch of sugar.

Mustards: I usually use Dijon mustard. It is very hot so add it carefully. When I was on holiday in Wales, I discovered another delicious mustard – this one whole grain, with honey and cider. I was having tea in a small stone cottage by the riverside, and was so impressed by the quality of the mustard that I ordered another turkey sandwich to enjoy it more. Now the man who makes the mustard sends me jars regularly in the post.

Pesto: This Italian sauce is made from basil, garlic, pine kernels (pine nuts), Parmesan and olive oil. I always keep a jar of it in my refrigerator.

Soy sauce: I use Japanese soy sauce in certain dishes as a lighter alternative to *jus de veau* – it is also more convenient unless you happen to have some *jus de veau* in the refrigerator or freezer. (Soy sauce will also be preferred by vegetarians.) Remember to be careful with the salt when you use soy sauce in a dish.

Tapenade: This mixture of anchovies, black olives, capers and olive oil is sold in small jars. It is beautiful as a canapé, spread on toast, and also to season a simple pan-fried fish, such as red mullet, with a squeeze of lemon juice.

OTHER INGREDIENTS

Mushrooms: When buying fresh button mushrooms, choose ones that are very firm. You can now find frozen mushrooms, which I think are very good – in fact, frozen mushrooms often have more flavour than week-old fresh button mushrooms. Fresh wild mushrooms, usually from France or Italy, are sold in some shops. It's a shame they aren't more widely available and that they are so expensive. Unfortunately, most of the wild mushrooms growing in Britain just feed the slugs! Dried wild mushrooms can be bought in delicatessens and other speciality food shops.

Truffles: Black truffles, usually from the Périgord in the southwest of France, are one of the most expensive items in French cuisine, costing about £150 a pound. I can remember my mother being paid with truffles for cooking the geese of a rich farmer. Black truffles grow near the roots of oak trees. They are not cultivated but are encouraged to grow. The other well-known truffles are the white ones from Piedmont in Italy, which are eaten raw, often grated over hot pasta. They have a very strong smell and are even more expensive: about £400 a pound! I would suggest you use black truffle peelings in your recipes. They are much less costly and are available here in cans. Avoid spring truffles because they have no flavour at all.

Tomatoes: My favourite is the plum-type tomato. When it is not in season, I suggest you substitute canned Italian tomatoes. I believe it is better to use a good canned tomato than a fresh one that is green, acidic and lacking in flavour.

Rocket or *arugula*: This salad green has long leaves with a strong, bitter taste. Only a few years ago it was very difficult to find, but now it is widely available in shops and supermarkets.

Sorrel: The leaves of this herb/vegetable look like spinach, and have a sour taste. Sorrel is especially good with fish.

Seaweed: I like adding seaweed to fish dishes. The ones I usually use are wakame or mekabu, but if you go to a Japanese or wholefood shop, you can find a wide range of dried edible seaweeds to try.

Pine kernels or *pine nuts*: These are the seeds from the cones of the stone pine. Use them like hazelnuts. They are particularly good toasted and added to salads.

Gelatine leaves: Look for these in the baking section of big stores and supermarkets. They are easier to use than powdered unflavoured gelatine because you don't need to worry that they won't dissolve completely. Vegetarians can substitute agar-agar.

Chocolate: I prefer to use Belgian or Swiss dark unsweetened or bitter sweet chocolate. Whatever chocolate you choose for desserts, always buy the best quality you can afford – it makes such a difference!

Pain d'épices: Made with honey and spices, this is a traditional afternoon tea bread for children in France. A good substitute here is Jamaica gingercake or Christmas or plum pudding, or any similar dark, moist and spicy cake.

Duck fat: This is still difficult to find in this country, so you may have to make your own: trim all the excess fat from a large duck, including the skin, place it in a large saucepan with an equal quantity of water and simmer until melted. Also, when you roast a duck, keep the fat in the roasting tin. Duck fat is excellent for flavouring sauté potatoes or a *potage*. Add a spoonful of duck fat at the end of cooking.

Cream: Double or heavy cream is what I normally use in cooking, although I don't ever use a lot, but if you are very worried about fat in your diet, you can use plain yogurt instead – adding it at the end of cooking or it will curdle.

A FEW TECHNIQUES
In preparing the recipes in this book, you will come across certain techniques over and over again. Most of these will be familiar to you, but some may not be, so here I give some simple instructions.

In the professional kitchen, all raw ingredients are prepared ahead of time, in quantity, so the dish can be cooked and finished as quickly as possible. This so-called *mise en place* is a good idea for the home cook, too, so that all the ingredients are ready and to hand when the cooking starts.

Cutting a 'julienne': peel the vegetable and cut it across into pieces 4 cm/1½ inches long. Cut the pieces lengthways into thin slices, 2 mm/ scant ⅛ inch thick. Place each slice flat and cut it lengthways into fine strips, or *juliennes*.

Turning vegetables: peel the vegetable and cut into quarters, then cut each quarter into pieces 5 cm/2 inches long. Trim the pieces to 2 cm/ ¾ inch thick. Place one piece in your left hand (if you are right-handed) and, using a small, sharp knife, trim all the angles to obtain a uniform barrel shape. The result is very pretty.

Turning vegetables will take quite a long time if you have not done it before, but the more you practise, the quicker it will be.

Shaping a 'quenelle': using two large spoons, dip them in warm water, then dip one spoon into the preparation to be shaped. Turn the spoons and scrape the mixture from one to the other six to eight times, finally making a neat three-sided oval or egg shape. Scrape this *quenelle* carefully on to the plate, with the help of the second spoon.

Zesting citrus fruit: you can use a vegetable peeler to take the zest, or coloured part of the peel, from oranges, lemons and so on and then cut it into strips or shreds. Or you can use a special citrus zester, which takes off the zest in fine threads. Dry citrus zest over a string in your kitchen and then store in jars; it will lend a beautiful aroma to your kitchen as well as to your food.

Blanching and refreshing: after blanching a vegetable in boiling water (or cooking it), drain it well in a colander and then plunge it into cold or iced water to stop the cooking and set the colour. In professional kitchens, vegetables are placed in wire baskets for blanching and cooking so they can easily be lifted from the boiling water into the iced water.

Deglazing: food that has been cooked in little or no fat – fried, sautéed, roasted and so on – will leave caramelised juices on the bottom of the pan. This sediment is full of flavour, so a liquid such as wine, vinegar or stock is added and the pan is deglazed by scraping and stirring in the sediment.

Enriching with butter: a smooth finish and shine is given to a sauce by adding a small piece of cold butter and swirling the sauce to mix in the butter as it melts. In French, this is called *monter au beurre*.

Resting meat: after roasting, all birds and pieces of meat should be allowed to rest for at least 10 minutes. During the cooking, the heat forces the juices into the centre of the meat; a period of resting lets the fibres relax so the juices can spread back evenly through the meat. Then when you carve the bird or meat, the juices will be retained making the meat more moist and flavoursome.

Seasoning: always test the seasoning of a dish by tasting it, now and again throughout the cooking and then finally just before serving (using a clean spoon). Be judicious when adding salt and pepper – many dishes do not need them at all and food is often over-seasoned in the kitchen. As a result, the palate grows accustomed to this and expects strong seasoning.

Notes for American cooks: In the recipes, cup and spoon measurements have been given where required (they appear as the third measure for each ingredient). Cup equivalents have not been used for foods usually sold by weight. Where the name of an ingredient or a term is different in the U.S., the equivalent is given in parenthesis.

SUGGESTED MENUS

SPRING

Caille rôtie en salade de coleslaw

Fricassée de saumon à l'étouffée de légumes et
vinaigre balsamique

Gâteau de fromage blanc, 'punch' de fruits

SUMMER

Gaspacho de saumon fumé

Solette rôtie à l'huile de crustacés et
tomates confites
Palets à l'ail
Fenouil braisé

Poires pochées au cassis, glace au lait d'amandes

AUTUMN

Ravioles de navets et champignons

Filet de chevreuil dans une sauce réglisse et
vin rouge
Purée d'hiver

Soufflé chaud au chocolat

WINTER

Potage d'artichauts et roquette

Queue de boeuf mijotée aux pruneaux et
au vinaigre
Petits choux farcis grand-mère or Purée d'hiver

Tarte à la molasse

SUNDAY LUNCH

Quiche soufflée de chou-fleur au bleu

Poulet des landes rôti à l'ail et au citron
'Gabaldi' provençale
Gratin dauphinois

Crème brûlée au citron

A SPECIAL OCCASION

Rillettes de crabe et morue

Homard rôti à l'orange et cardamome

Confit de canard au vin aux figues
Fenouil braisé

Mille feuille de chocolat aux cerises

MY CHILDREN'S FAVOURITES

Oeufs cocotte à la ratatouille safranée

Parmentier de canard
Salade 'favorite' or a green salad

Îles flottantes

MY CHOICE

Tatin de céléri aux truffes du Périgord

Escalope de foie de veau Mauricette
Spätzels or boiled potatoes

Figues confites à l'anis, parfait
à la verveine

Fond blanc de volaille

Jus de veau

Nage de légumes

Fumet de poisson

Sauce verte girondine

Sauce mousse tartare

Crème de raifort et muscade

Pâtes fraîches

Sauce rapide pour les pâtes

Mayonnaise

Vinaigrette

Glaçage à rôtis

Sauce rapide pour grillades (viandes et poissons)

Huile de crustacés

Crème anglaise

CHAPTER ONE

Les Bases

BASICS

The recipes here are for items useful to have at hand because they are used in or with so many other dishes: pasta dough, basic stocks, glazes, a flavoured oil, and sweet and savoury sauces.

FOND BLANC DE VOLAILLE
White Chicken Stock

2 kg/4½ lb raw chicken bones, or equivalent in boiling fowl
(stewing chicken)
½ teaspoon salt
200 g/7 oz onions
200 g/7 oz white part of leeks
100 g/3½ oz celery
4 cloves of garlic
a bunch of fresh thyme
a bunch of fresh parsley
½ bay leaf
1 clove
½ teaspoon white peppercorns

P UT the chicken bones in a large, deep saucepan or stockpot. Cover with cold water and add the salt. Bring to the boil, skimming the impurities and scum off the surface as they form.

Peel the onions. Cut all the vegetables into chunks. Add the vegetables to the pan with the remaining ingredients and leave to simmer for 1 hour.

Strain the stock through a fine sieve. Cool until completely cold, then keep in the refrigerator until ready to use. (It can be kept for 3–4 days.)

BRUNO'S NOTES

You can make this stock well in advance, and freeze it in usuable quantities in plastic bags.

To make a nice sauce for white meat, reduce some stock, add some double cream (heavy cream) and reduce it a bit, then add cooked mushrooms and a dash of tarragon vinegar.

JUS DE VEAU
Veal Stock

MAKES 2 litres/3½ pints/2 quarts

150 ml/5 fl oz vegetable oil
1 kg/2¼ lb veal trimmings, preferably fatty ones from the breast
100 ml/3½ fl oz tarragon vinegar
500 g/1 lb 2 oz/2½ cups canned tomatoes (drained weight)
400 g/14 oz onions
200 g/7 oz carrots
100 g/3½ oz celery
100 g/3½ oz mushrooms
5 cloves of garlic
a bunch of fresh thyme
a few parsley stems (about 10)
¼ bay leaf

BRUNO'S NOTES

You can store the stock in containers or bags in your freezer. Or reduce it to 500 ml/16 fl oz to obtain a *glace de veau* (veal essence) and chill in the refrigerator until set, then cut into cubes, wrap separately and freeze.

IN a large roasting tin, heat 100 ml / 3½ fl oz of the oil until very hot. Add the veal trimmings and stir well with a wooden spoon to mix with the oil, then turn the heat down and cook until the meat has exuded all of its juices. These will then caramelise and become sticky and golden. Deglaze the tin with the vinegar and the tomatoes, stirring well to mix with the caramelised juices. Remove from the heat and put aside.

Peel the onions and carrots; cut them into large dice along with the celery and mushrooms. In a large heavy saucepan, heat the remaining oil and add the vegetables. Cook on a moderate heat until they are lightly browned, stirring occasionally. Pour in 4 litres/7 pints/4 quarts of water and add the veal mixture, the halved garlic cloves and the herbs. Bring to the boil, then leave to simmer for 2½ hours, skimming from time to time.

Strain the stock through a colander and then through a fine sieve.

NAGE DE LÉGUMES
Vegetable Stock

MAKES 1 litre/1¾ pints/1 quart

100 g/3½ oz onions
90 g/3 oz carrots
90 g/3 oz leeks
60 g/2 oz bulb of fennel
90 g/3 oz celery
2 cloves of garlic
a bunch of fresh thyme
1 star anise
1 teaspoon coriander seeds
4 black peppercorns
¼ bay leaf
½ lemon
a bunch of fresh tarragon
a bunch of fresh parsley
100 ml/3½ fl oz dry white wine

BRUNO'S NOTES

This stock is an excellent medium for poaching fish and shellfish. It can also be made into a quick, delicate sauce for fish: boil 100 ml/ 3½ fl oz of nage and add 2 tablespoons of double cream (heavy cream). Reduce the heat and whisk in 30 g/1 oz/ 2 tablespoons of cold unsalted butter, in small pieces. Add snipped fresh dill or basil and some diced tomato flesh, and serve.

PEEL or trim all the vegetables, then chop them very finely. Put them in a large saucepan together with the thyme, star anise, coriander seeds, lightly crushed peppercorns and bay leaf. Add 1 litre/1¾ pints/1 quart of cold water. Bring to the boil and simmer for about 12 minutes.

Slice the lemon half and add it to the pan with the tarragon and parsley. Leave to simmer for a further 3 minutes.

Remove from the heat, put a lid on the pan and leave to infuse in a cool place overnight.

The next day, strain the stock through a colander and then through a fine sieve. Stir in the wine. Nage de légumes can be stored in the refrigerator in a glass or stainless steel container for at least 3 days.

FUMET DE POISSON
Fish Stock

MAKES 1 litre/1¾ pints/1 quart

500 g/1 lb 2 oz fish bones and heads from brill, sole or whiting
100 g/3½ oz onions
75 g/2½ oz leeks
75 g/2½ oz celery
75 g/2½ oz bulb of fennel
200 ml/7 fl oz dry white wine
6 coriander seeds
4 black peppercorns
a branch of fresh thyme

R INSE the fish bones and heads under cold running water for 5 minutes to clean them thoroughly.

Peel or trim the onions, leeks, celery and fennel, then finely chop all these vegetables. In a large saucepan, combine the chopped vegetables, the wine, spices and thyme. Bring to the boil and boil for 5 minutes, then add the fish bones and heads. Cover with 1 litre/1¾ pints/1 quart of cold water. Bring back to the boil, skimming the surface to remove all the scum and impurities, then leave to simmer for 15 minutes.

Strain the stock through a fine sieve, and use as required.

BRUNO'S NOTES

You can store this stock in the refrigerator in a covered container for 3 or 4 days, and you can freeze it as well.

SAUCE VERTE GIRONDINE
Green Sauce Girondine-Style

SERVES 4-6

90 g/3 oz shallots, preferably pink
3½ tablespoons red wine vinegar
½ tablespoon finely chopped garlic
100 ml/3½ fl oz olive oil
1 tablespoon chopped fresh tarragon
1 tablespoon chopped fresh parsley
1 tablespoon chopped fresh chervil
½ tablespoon chopped fresh basil
salt and freshly ground black pepper

P EEL the shallots and chop them very finely. Put the shallots in a small bowl with the vinegar, garlic and oil.

In a small pan, boil 5 tablespoons of water. Stir in all the herbs. Mix this quickly into the ingredients in the bowl, season to taste, and serve.

BRUNO'S NOTES

This sauces goes well with grilled fish or meat, but is particularly good with boiled fish or meat.

SAUCE MOUSSE TARTARE
Tartare Sauce with Cream

SERVES 4

30 g/1 oz onion, shallot or red onion
1 hard-boiled egg
1 egg yolk
1 teaspoon Dijon mustard
salt and freshly ground black pepper
100 ml/3½ fl oz vegetable oil
1 tablespoon tarragon vinegar
1 teaspoon chopped gherkin or cornichon
1 teaspoon chopped capers
1 tablespoon chopped fresh parsley
125 ml/4 fl oz whipping cream

PEEL and finely chop the onion. Shell and chop the hard-boiled egg. Put the raw egg yolk and mustard in a bowl and mix very well together with a whisk. Season with 2 pinches of salt and a pinch of pepper. Slowly pour in the oil, whisking constantly, to obtain a nice, thick mayonnaise. Add the tarragon vinegar together with all the chopped ingredients and mix well.

In another bowl, whip the cream until stiff. Fold it into the mayonnaise using a large spoon while rotating the bowl. Keep the sauce in the refrigerator until ready to serve. It is excellent with cold meat.

CRÈME DE RAIFORT ET MUSCADE
Horseradish and Nutmeg Cream

BRUNO'S NOTES

This is a very nice dip for crudités as well as an excellent sauce for poached fish.

SERVES 4

125 ml/4 fl oz whipping cream
1 tablespoon horseradish sauce
4 spring onions (scallions)
60 g/2 oz radishes
1 tablespoon chopped fresh chives
freshly grated nutmeg
Tabasco sauce
salt and freshly ground black pepper

WHIP the cream until it is thick but not stiff, then add the horseradish sauce. Trim and finely chop the spring onions and radishes. Add to the cream with the chives, and nutmeg, Tabasco, salt and pepper to taste.

PÂTES FRAÎCHES
Fresh Pasta Dough

MAKES 300 g/10 oz

250 g/9 oz/1⅔ cups flour
3 pinches of salt
4 egg yolks
1 whole egg
a drop of white wine vinegar
1 tablespoon olive oil

PUT all the ingredients into a food processor and mix for 30 seconds or until you obtain a ball of dough that leaves the sides of the processor bowl clean. You may need to add a little bit of water, depending on the size of the eggs and the quality of the flour. (If you don't have a food processor, you can, of course, mix the ingredients together by hand.)

Place the dough on a lightly floured surface and knead until you get a nice smooth, elastic consistency. Wrap and chill in the refrigerator for at least 1 hour.

Cut the dough into 4 equal pieces. Flatten with a rolling pin and pass each piece through the pasta machine, according to the manufacturer's instructions. If you don't have a pasta machine, you can roll out the dough using the rolling pin, but you will need a lot of patience as it will take much longer to achieve a sheet of dough that is very thin and almost transparent.

BRUNO'S NOTES

You can dry the pasta if you don't want to use it immediately. Put it on a floured tray or hang it over a floured wooden stick, such as a clean broomhandle. Or freeze the fresh pasta in a plastic container or on a tray covered very tightly.

To give the pasta a light yellow colour, add a pinch of saffron dissolved in a little water.

SAUCE RAPIDE POUR LES PÂTES
Simple Sauce for Pasta

SERVES 4

60 g/2 oz onion
60 g/2 oz ripe tomatoes, preferably plum-type
3½ tablespoons olive oil
1 clove of garlic
1 tablespoon pesto
2 anchovy fillets

PEEL and chop the onion. Cut the tomatoes in half and discard the seeds, then chop the tomatoes.

In a sauté pan, heat the oil and soften the onion for 2 minutes, then add the finely chopped garlic and the tomatoes. Cook for 5 minutes, stirring occasionally.

Stir in the pesto and the anchovy fillets cut into very small pieces.

BRUNO'S NOTES

This is extremely quick and easy, and is delicious with any pasta.

You can replace the anchovy fillets with 1 teaspoon tapenade, or more to taste.

MAYONNAISE

MAKES 250 ml/8 fl oz

2 egg yolks
2 teaspoons Dijon mustard
salt and freshly ground white pepper
200 ml/7 fl oz grapeseed or other mild oil
1 teaspoon lemon juice
1 tablespoon white wine vinegar

IN a large mixing bowl, whisk together the egg yolks, mustard, 3 pinches of salt and a pinch of pepper. Add the oil gradually, whisking energetically. When the mixture has thickened and all the oil has been absorbed, add the lemon juice and vinegar and whisk well. Correct the seasoning to your taste.

BRUNO'S NOTES

You can store the mayonnaise in a covered container in the lower part of the refrigerator, but not longer than 3 days as the egg yolks are raw.

VINAIGRETTE

MAKES 250 ml/8 fl oz

3½ tablespoons white wine vinegar
1 teaspoon Dijon mustard
salt and freshly ground black pepper
200 ml/7 fl oz vegetable oil

MIX the vinegar with the mustard, 2 large pinches of salt and a small pinch of pepper in a small bottle or jar. Add the oil, and cover the bottle or jar. Keep in the refrigerator. Shake well just before using the dressing.

BRUNO'S NOTES

For a hazelnut or walnut vinaigrette, use 3½ tablespoons of nut-scented oil and 150 ml/5 fl oz vegetable oil.

For an olive oil vinaigrette, use 150 ml/5 fl oz olive oil and 3½ tablespoons vegetable oil, and add ½ clove of garlic, crushed with the side of a knife.

GLAÇAGE À RÔTIS
Glaze for Roasts

120 g/4 oz/6 tablespoons liquid honey
3 tablespoons tomato paste
2 tablespoons soy sauce
3 tablespoons red wine vinegar

MIX all the ingredients together and put in a jar. Cover tightly. This will keep very well in the refrigerator.

BRUNO'S NOTES

This simple glaze will transform a plain roast of pork or poultry such as chicken or turkey – particularly a bird of inferior quality. Spread it on for the last 10 minutes of roasting, and turn the oven temperature down slightly so that the honey in the glaze doesn't burn.

SAUCE RAPIDE POUR GRILLADES
Quick Sauce for Meat or Fish

SERVES 4

FOR MEAT
1 clove of garlic
125 ml/4 fl oz plain yogurt
1 tablespoon tandoori paste
1 tablespoon horseradish cream
1 tablespoon HP Sauce
1 tablespoon chopped fresh parsley
1 teaspoon malt vinegar

FOR FISH
1 tablespoon pesto
1 tablespoon mint sauce
1 tablespoon olive oil
juice of ½ lemon
2 tablespoons tomato juice

TO make the quick sauce for meat, peel and finely chop the garlic and mix with the remaining ingredients.

To make the quick sauce for fish, mix all the ingredients together.

Spread the sauce over the meat or fish being grilled (broiled) or barbecued when it is about three-quarters cooked, in time for it to bubble and brown.

BRUNO'S NOTES

These sauces are made from ingredients you probably have on hand in the refrigerator and storecupboard. They need almost no preparation, and can be a great help to a busy cook.

HUILE DE CRUSTACÉS
Shellfish Oil

300 ml/10 fl oz olive oil
450 g/1 lb shells from very briefly blanched lobsters, langoustines
or crayfish or uncooked king prawns (jumbo shrimp)
1 tablespoon tomato paste
2 cloves of garlic
20 g/⅔ oz fresh root ginger
a strip of orange zest

IN a large saucepan, heat 200 ml/7 fl oz of the olive oil until hot, then add the shells and cook on a low heat for 5 minutes. Stir in the tomato paste, garlic crushed with the side of a knife, the chopped ginger and orange zest. Leave to cook for 2 minutes, then remove from the heat. Add the remaining oil and set aside to infuse for 2 hours. Then strain the oil through a fine sieve and pour into bottles. Store in the refrigerator.

BRUNO'S NOTES

You can use the shells from the lobsters that have been cooked by the fishmonger, but the oil will not have as much flavour or colour.

Use this flavoured oil to dress a shellfish salad or even a grilled fish, with some lemon juice to taste.

CRÈME ANGLAISE
Vanilla Cream

SERVES 4–8, according to use

6 egg yolks
75 g/2½ oz/6 tablespoons caster sugar (U.S. granulated sugar)
500 ml/16 fl oz creamy milk
½ vanilla pod (vanilla bean), or ½ tablespoon vanilla essence
(vanilla extract)

IN a large bowl, mix together the egg yolks and sugar with a whisk until you obtain a white, creamy consistency.

Put the milk and vanilla pod in a heavy-based saucepan (if using vanilla essence, add it later). Heat until the milk boils and rises in the pan, then remove from the heat and pour the milk over the egg and sugar mixture, whisking constantly. Return the mixture to the saucepan and cook on medium heat, stirring constantly with a wooden spoon, until the cream thickens and will coat the back of the spoon. Don't let the cream boil.

Strain quickly through a fine sieve into a cold bowl. If using vanilla essence, add it now. When the cream is cold, cover and put it into the refrigerator.

BRUNO'S NOTES

This cream is the base of or accompaniment for many desserts, and it can be flavoured with different liqueurs, orange zest, chocolate and so on.

It is important that the milk be boiling before it is added to the egg yolks so that the heat of the milk will start to cook the yolks immediately, and help to kill any harmful microorganisms that might be present in the eggs. After the egg yolks have been added, the cream must not be boiled or it will curdle.

Velouté de chou-fleur infusé au cumin

Potage de potiron et gnocchis à la muscade

Potage d'artichauts et roquette

Gaspacho de saumon fumé

Consommé de cailles et miques aux cèpes

Saumon mariné sur l'assiette

Tourin blanc du Sud-Ouest au confit

Ravioles de navets et champignons

Coquilles St Jacques à la grecque de légumes

Oeufs cocotte à la ratatouille safranée

Quiche soufflée de chou-fleur au bleu

Endives en surprise

Salade 'favorite'

Canellonis de poireaux aux pignons de pins

Tatin de céleri aux truffes du Périgord

Rillettes de crabe et morue

Assiette de fruits de mer, petits légumes en gelée, crème d'artichauts à l'huile d'olive

Pizza de champignons

Salade de M. Vinicio

Terrine de cailles aux abricots secs

Moules marinières au cresson

Gros ravioles d'escargots, salade de coeurs de laitue aux lardons

Caille rôtie en salade de coleslaw

Terrine de petit salé, purée de pois cassés

Terrine du pauvre

CHAPTER TWO

Hors d'Oeuvre

FIRST COURSES

The first course is the introduction to the meal. It should not be too much, or the appetite will be spoiled, and should complement or contrast with the following dish in the menu. When choosing a first course, also keep in mind the time needed to prepare it, particularly at the last minute when other things might need attention. Many of these first courses can be adapted to make a main course for a light supper. I very much enjoy a dish like this on my evenings off because it is usually simple and quick to prepare (and my wife does not complain). Bon appetit.

VELOUTÉ DE CHOU-FLEUR INFUSÉ AU CUMIN

Cream of Cauliflower Soup Flavoured with Cumin

SERVES 4

100 g/3½ oz onions
75 g/2½ oz white part of leeks
60 g/2 oz/4 tablespoons unsalted butter
500 ml/16 fl oz milk
salt and freshly ground white pepper
freshly grated nutmeg
1 clove of garlic
1 teaspoon cumin seeds
400 g/14 oz cauliflower
100 ml/3½ fl oz double cream (heavy cream)
60 g/2 oz emmental or Parmesan cheese

PEEL and chop the onions; trim and chop the leeks. In a deep heavy-based saucepan, melt the butter over a low heat and sweat the onions and leeks, covered, until soft, without colouring. Add the milk, a little salt, 2 pinches of nutmeg and the finely chopped garlic. Tie the cumin seeds in a small piece of muslin or cheesecloth and put into the soup. Bring to the boil, then add the cauliflower cut into pieces. Cover and cook over a low heat for 30 minutes.

Take the muslin bag out and discard it. Liquidise the soup in a blender until smooth. Pour into a clean pan, add the cream and salt and pepper to taste, and reheat.

Ladle the soup into individual flameproof soup bowls. Top with the grated cheese and place under a preheated hot grill (broiler) to melt and brown the cheese. Serve immediately.

BRUNO'S NOTES

If you are in a cooking mood, make a cheese soufflé, then top each portion of soup with a scoop of soufflé rather than the gratinéed cheese, and serve immediately.

POTAGE DE POTIRON ET GNOCCHIS À LA MUSCADE

Creamed Pumpkin Soup Garnished with Nutmeg Gnocchi

SERVES 4

500 g/1 lb 2 oz pumpkin flesh (peeled, seeded weight)
100 g/3½ oz onions
100 g/3½ oz carrots
60 g/2 oz/4 tablespoons unsalted butter
60 g/2 oz tomatoes, preferably plum-type
500 ml/16 fl oz milk
salt and freshly ground white pepper
a bunch of fresh chives

GNOCCHI
150 g/5 oz peeled potatoes
1 egg
200 ml/7 fl oz milk
30 g/1 oz/3 tablespoons flour
15 g/½ oz/1 tablespoon unsalted butter
1 teaspoon freshly grated Parmesan cheese
salt and freshly ground black pepper
freshly grated nutmeg

PREHEAT the oven to 150°C/300°F/gas mark 2.

First make the gnocchi. Cut the potatoes into large cubes and cook in boiling salted water until tender – about 25 minutes. Drain well in a colander, then spread out in a baking tin. Put into the oven for about 10 minutes to dry.

Pass the potatoes through a mouli, coarse sieve or potato ricer into a bowl. Blend the egg, milk and flour thoroughly together, then add to the potatoes with the butter and Parmesan. Season with salt, pepper and nutmeg. Work the mixture with a wooden spoon to obtain a firm dough. With the hands, roll into small hazelnut-sized balls.

Cook the gnocchi in boiling salted water for 2 minutes. Remove with a slotted spoon and leave to drain on paper towels.

To make the soup, cut the pumpkin into cubes, and peel and chop the onions and carrots. In a large saucepan, melt the butter and sweat the pumpkin, onions and carrots over a low heat for about 10 minutes without letting them colour. Remove the seeds from the tomatoes and chop them, then add to the pan with the milk. Season with salt and pepper. Leave to simmer gently for about 30 minutes, stirring occasionally.

Liquidise the soup until smooth, then pass it through a fine sieve into a clean pan. Add the gnocchi and reheat for 5 minutes. Ladle the soup into hot soup plates and sprinkle over some chopped chives. Serve hot.

POTAGE D'ARTICHAUTS ET ROQUETTE
Creamed Artichoke and Rocket Soup

SERVES 4

2 globe artichokes
½ lemon
salt and freshly ground white pepper
150 g/5 oz Jerusalem artichokes
60 g/2 oz onion
100 g/3½ oz white part of leeks
a handful of rocket (arugula) leaves
60 g/2 oz/4 tablespoons unsalted butter
200 ml/7 fl oz dry white wine
100 ml/3½ fl oz double cream (heavy cream)

CUT the stalks off the globe artichokes with a sharp knife. Starting from the base, cut off all the leaves by turning the artichokes round, until you are left with just the bottom or *fond*. Put the bottoms into a pan of water. Squeeze the juice from the lemon half into the water and add the lemon half with 1 teaspoon of salt. Cut out a round of greaseproof or parchment paper to fit inside the pan, and cut a steam hole in the centre of the paper round. Place the paper on the water's surface. Bring to the boil, then simmer for 20 minutes or until the artichoke bottoms are tender (test with the tip of a sharp knife).

Meanwhile, peel the Jerusalem artichokes and leave them in water to cover, to prevent discoloration. Peel and finely chop the onion; trim and finely chop the leeks. Trim and rinse the rocket leaves in cold water as you would a lettuce. Drain well, then shred the rocket roughly.

In a heavy-based saucepan, melt half of the butter with 2 tablespoons of water over low heat and sweat the onion and leeks, covered, until soft, without colouring.

Drain the globe artichoke bottoms and remove the hairy chokes with a teaspoon or your thumb. Add the artichokes to the leeks and onion together with the wine and drained Jerusalem artichokes. Add enough cold water so the vegetables are just covered with liquid. Bring to the boil, then simmer for 15 minutes.

Stir in the cream and salt and pepper to taste. Liquidise in a blender until smooth, then pass through a very fine sieve into a clean saucepan. If the soup is too thick, add a little bit of milk. Bring the soup to the boil, then add the rocket and remaining butter cut into small pieces. Cook for another 2 minutes, stirring, and serve.

BRUNO'S NOTES

Large, coarse rocket leaves have a stronger flavour than those that are young and tender. If you can get small leaves, use a large handful.

If you want to serve this soup for a special occasion, add some diced smoked salmon at the last moment before serving. You will then have the most delicious soup you have ever tasted.

GASPACHO DE SAUMON FUMÉ
Gaspacho of Smoked Salmon

SERVES 4

200 g/7 oz smoked salmon
2 stalks of celery
500 g/1 lb 2 oz ripe plum-type tomatoes
½ cucumber
salt
½ clove of garlic
½ slice of white bread
2 tablespoons red wine vinegar
celery salt
Tabasco sauce
1 tablespoon olive oil
4 leaves of fresh basil

CUT the smoked salmon into very small dice and put aside in the refrigerator. Do the same thing with the celery. Cut the tomatoes in half and remove the seeds by squeezing the halves over a bowl.

Peel the cucumber and cut it in half lengthways. Scoop out the seeds with a teaspoon, being careful not to take any flesh, then slice across very finely. Put in a bowl, sprinkle with salt and leave for 10 minutes. Then rinse under cold running water and spread out on paper towels to dry.

Put the tomatoes, peeled garlic, half the cucumber, the bread and vinegar in a food processor and process for 30 seconds. Pass through a very fine sieve into a bowl and season to taste with celery salt and Tabasco sauce. Whisk in the olive oil. Cover and chill for about 30 minutes.

Line the inside of a small ladle with cucumber slices, arranging them so they are slightly overlapping. Press one-quarter of the diced salmon and celery and chopped basil into the hollow. Turn upside-down to unmould and place in the centre of a soup plate. Repeat with the other plates. Whisk the gaspacho briefly, then pour it around the salmon moulds and serve.

BRUNO'S NOTES

This is an excellent first course for sunny days before a barbecue. At the Inn on the Park, I replace the cucumber slices with thin slices of scallops poached in Noilly Prat.

Illustrated on PLATE 3

SALADE 'FAVORITE'

My Favourite Salad

SERVES 4

200 g/7 oz watercress
150 g/5 oz curly endive (frisé)
150 g/5 oz chicory (Belgian endive)
90 g/3 oz cooked beetroot (beets)
1 Granny Smith apple
75 g/2½ oz spring onions (scallions)
90 g/3 oz goat's cheese or Roquefort
1 tablespoon red wine vinegar
2 tablespoons walnut oil
1 tablespoon vegetable oil
freshly ground black pepper
100 g/3½ oz unsmoked streaky bacon (slices of
mild-cure bacon or salt pork)

PICK over the watercress and curly endive, discarding wilted or discoloured leaves and thick stalks. Separate the chicory leaves. Peel and dice the beetroot. Core the apple and cut into large *julienne*. Chop the spring onions. Cut the cheese into small pieces.

In a large salad bowl, combine the vinegar, oils and pepper to taste, mixing with a whisk or fork.

Remove the rind from the bacon rashers, if necessary, then cut them across into small *lardons*. Sauté them in a non-stick frying pan until crisp. Drain them on paper towels.

Add all the prepared ingredients to the salad bowl, toss with the dressing, and serve.

Illustrated opposite

Salade 'Favorite'

My Favourite Salad

PLATE 1

Coquilles St Jacques à la Grecque de Légumes

Grilled Scallops with Marinated Vegetables
(recipe page 36)

PLATE 2

Gaspacho de Saumon Fumé

———————

Gaspacho of Smoked Salmon
(recipe page 31)

PLATE 3

Canellonis de Poireaux aux Pignons de Pins

Leek and Pine Kernel Canelloni

PLATE 4

CANELLONIS DE POIREAUX AUX PIGNONS DE PINS

Leek and Pine Kernel Canelloni

SERVES 4

4 large leeks
60 g/2 oz white mushrooms
100 ml/3½ fl oz double cream (heavy cream)
1 tablespoon chopped fresh chervil
1 tablespoon chopped fresh tarragon
1 tablespoon chopped fresh parsley
a slice of white bread
3 tablespoons milk
1 egg
50 g/1¾ oz/½ cup pine kernels (pine nuts)
100 ml/3½ fl oz Nage de Légumes (page 19)
45 g/1½ oz/3 tablespoons cold unsalted butter
salt and freshly ground black pepper
¼ lemon
fresh herbs to garnish

TRIM and clean the leeks and cut them into 8 cm/3¼ inch lengths. Slit them open lengthways. Blanch the leeks in boiling salted water for 5 minutes; drain and refresh under cold running water. Reserve 16 large leaves and chop the rest. Chop the mushrooms.

Put all but 1 tablespoon of the cream in a flat pan and bring to the boil. Add the chopped leeks and mushrooms and reduce until very thick and syrupy. Add the chopped herbs and cook, stirring, for 2 minutes. Pour this mixture into a bowl and leave to cool.

Break the bread into pieces and put in a small bowl. Add the milk and mash with a fork, then mix into the leek and herb mixture with the egg.

Toast the pine kernels under the grill (broiler) until they are nicely golden all over, shaking the pan so that they brown evenly. Reserve 20 g/ ⅔ oz/about 3 tablespoons of the pine kernels for the garnish, and add the rest to the leek and herb mixture.

Lay 2 leek leaves side by side, slightly overlapping, on a sheet of greased foil. Top with 2 tablespoons of the leek and herb mixture and roll into a sausage shape, twisting the foil at both ends to secure it tightly. Repeat to make 8 canelloni.

Place the canelloni in a steamer and cook for 8 minutes.

Meanwhile, put the nage in a small saucepan and bring to the boil. Drop in the reserved tablespoon of cream. Remove from the heat and whisk in the butter, in small pieces. Season to taste with salt and pepper and add a squeeze of lemon juice.

To serve, place the canelloni in the centre of hot plates and spoon the sauce round. Sprinkle over some fresh herbs and the reserved pine kernels.

Illustrated opposite

TOURIN BLANC DU SUD-OUEST AU CONFIT

Onion Soup with Duck Confit

SERVES 4

200 g/7 oz onions
45 g/1½ oz duck fat, or 4 tablespoons grapeseed or other mild oil
a bunch of fresh thyme
1 leg of duck confit, weighing about 200 g/7 oz
(see recipe for Confit de Canard au Vin aux Figues, page 86)
45 g/1½ oz garlic
½ bay leaf
100 ml/3½ oz dry white wine
750 ml/1¼ pints/3 cups Fond Blanc de Volaille (page 18)
celery salt
freshly ground black pepper
1 egg
1 tablespoon chopped fresh chives

PEEL and thinly slice the onions. Heat the duck fat or oil in a saucepan and add the onions, thyme and 2 tablespoons of water. Cook over a low heat for about 10 minutes, stirring from time to time with a wooden spoon, until the onions become quite soft. Do not let them turn brown.

Meanwhile, peel the skin from the duck confit and take the meat off the bones. Cut each piece of meat into 2 or 3 pieces.

Add the sliced garlic, bay leaf and wine to the saucepan and stir for 2 minutes, then stir in the chicken stock (or water) and the duck confit. Simmer for 15 minutes.

Season to taste with celery salt and pepper, then remove the pan from the heat. With a fork, beat the egg and whisk it quickly into the hot soup.

To serve, ladle the soup into soup bowls and sprinkle over the chives.

BRUNO'S NOTES

My mother used to make this soup for us after a day's work in the vineyard.

RAVIOLES DE NAVETS ET CHAMPIGNONS
Turnip and Wild Mushroom Ravioli

SERVES 4

300 g/10 oz mixed fresh wild mushrooms
1 large, hard turnip, weighing about 350 g/12 oz
vegetable oil
salt and freshly ground black pepper
4 teaspoons mixed chopped fresh parsley and tarragon
tarragon vinegar
45 g/1½ oz/3 tablespoons unsalted butter
2 tablespoons soy sauce
fresh herbs such as chives, chervil and dill, to garnish

BRUNO'S NOTES

You can replace the wild mushrooms with a mixture of 300 g/10 oz white button mushrooms, sliced, and 45 g/1½ oz dried morels. You will need to soak the morels in warm water for 30 minutes and then clean them thoroughly under cold running water to remove all sandy grit.

If you prefer, the ravioli can be heated in a steamer rather than in the oven. Choose a plate that will fit into the steamer and arrange the ravioli on it in layers, leaving spaces around and between them so that the steam can penetrate.

TRIM and clean the wild mushrooms. Set aside.

Peel the turnip and slice it widthways very finely into paper-thin leaves. Use a mandoline for this operation as it is impossible to cut thin enough slices using a knife. From each slice of turnip, cut out a 6 cm/2½ inch diameter round. You should have 48 rounds.

Preheat the oven to 180°C/350°F/gas mark 4.

Heat a film of oil in a saucepan and add 200 g/7 oz of the mushrooms. Cook gently so that the water from the mushrooms will evaporate. Season with salt and pepper, and add 3 teaspoons of mixed parsley and tarragon. Continue to cook for 3–4 minutes, stirring occasionally.

Drain the mushrooms in a colander placed over a bowl to catch the juices. On a chopping board, chop the mushrooms very finely.

Cook the turnip rounds in boiling salted water with a drop of tarragon vinegar added for about 30 seconds. Drain and put immediately into iced water to stop the cooking. Pat the turnip rounds dry with paper towels.

Lay out half of the turnip rounds on the work surface and place a spoonful of the chopped mushrooms on the centre of each. Cover with the remaining turnip rounds, placing them neatly on top and pressing the edges together to seal.

Wet 2 clean linen towels and place one on a baking sheet. Arrange the turnip ravioli in one layer on the towel and cover with the second towel (or use a large towel, folded in half).

Melt the butter in a sauté pan, add the remaining wild mushrooms and sauté over a brisk heat for 3 minutes, stirring frequently. Keep hot.

Place the ravioli in the oven and heat for 3–4 minutes. Keep checking to be sure that the towels don't start to singe!

Meanwhile, in a small pan, warm the soy sauce with the mushroom juices and the remaining mixed parsley and tarragon.

To serve, arrange the ravioli on hot plates, pour the sauce over carefully and garnish with the sautéed mushrooms and a few fresh herbs.

COQUILLES ST JACQUES À LA GRECQUE DE LÉGUMES

Grilled Scallops with Marinated Vegetables

SERVES 4

60 g/2 oz shallots
100 ml/3½ fl oz olive oil
1 teaspoon coriander seeds
100 ml/3½ fl oz dry white wine
1 teaspoon tomato paste
2 cloves of garlic
ground cumin (optional)
150 g/5 oz/1¼ cups button onions (pearl onions)
100 g/3½ oz/1 cup cauliflower florets
60 g/2 oz button mushrooms
75 g/2½ oz tomatoes, preferably plum-type
10 large scallops (sea scallops)
salt and freshly ground black pepper
1 tablespoon finely snipped fresh coriander (cilantro)

BRUNO'S NOTES

For a dish like this you need a good quality olive oil, such as an extra virgin (first pressing) olive oil. I would choose an Italian olive oil as I find the Spanish and Greek olive oils too bitter.

PEEL the shallots and chop very finely. Heat a film of olive oil in a sauté pan, add the shallots and coriander seeds and cook on a moderate heat for about 3 minutes. Deglaze the pan with the white wine, stirring well, then stir in the tomato paste, garlic crushed with the side of a knife, and a pinch of cumin. Leave to simmer for 5 minutes.

Peel the button onions and put into the pan with 100 ml/3½ fl oz of water. Stir to mix. Cover and leave to cook gently for 8–10 minutes.

Add the cauliflower florets and continue to cook, covered, for 8 minutes, then add the mushrooms and cook for 5 minutes longer. Remove from the heat and leave to cool completely.

Skin and seed the tomatoes and cut the flesh into small dice. Set aside.

Brush each scallop on both sides with olive oil and season with salt and pepper. Heat a cast-iron grill pan until very hot, then put on the scallops and grill for 1 minute on each side.

Using a slotted spoon, arrange the vegetables on hot plates, then moisten each serving with 1 tablespoon of the juices. Cut the scallops in half lengthways and place around the vegetables. Sprinkle over the fresh coriander and diced tomatoes, add a few drops of olive oil to each plate and serve.

Illustrated on PLATE 2

OEUFS COCOTTE À LA RATATOUILLE SAFRANÉE

Eggs in Ramekins with a Saffron-Scented Ratatouille

BRUNO'S NOTES

If fresh plum-type tomatoes
are not available, you can use
canned tomatoes instead.
Drain the juice from a 400 g/
14 oz can of whole peeled
tomatoes, then remove the
seeds and chop the tomatoes.

This is a very simple,
cheap and tasty first course.

SERVES 4

100 g/3½ oz onions
100 g/3½ oz red sweet peppers
100 g/3½ oz courgettes (zucchini)
100 g/3½ oz aubergine (eggplant)
100 g/3½ oz plum-type tomatoes
3 tablespoons olive oil
2 cloves of garlic
a bouquet garni
saffron powder
salt and freshly ground black pepper
fresh basil (optional)
4 eggs

PEEL the onions; trim the sweet peppers, courgettes and aubergine. Cut the prepared vegetables into 5 mm/¼ inch dice. Skin, seed and chop the tomatoes.

In a frying pan, heat 2 tablespoons olive oil and cook the onions and sweet peppers for about 6 minutes, stirring occasionally, until soft. Remove with a slotted spoon and drain on paper towels. Add the remaining oil to the pan and heat it, then cook the courgettes and aubergine for 4 minutes or until soft. Drain on paper towels.

In a deep pan, mix together all the cooked vegetables, the tomatoes, garlic crushed with the side of a knife, and the bouquet garni. Season with a good pinch of saffron, and salt and pepper to taste. Pour in a wineglass of water. Simmer for 5 minutes. Discard the bouquet garni. If liked, stir in some chopped basil.

Divide the ratatouille among 4 ramekin dishes. Break an egg into each dish over the ratatouille. Place the dishes in a shallow, heavy-based pan and add boiling water to the pan to come three-quarters up the sides of the ramekins. Simmer gently until the egg whites are set but the yolks are still a little soft, 6–8 minutes.

Grind some pepper over the eggs and serve, with toast fingers.

QUICHE SOUFFLÉE DE CHOU-FLEUR AU BLEU

Blue Cheese and Cauliflower Soufflé Quiche

SERVES 4

250 g/9 oz/2¼ cups cauliflower florets
25 g/¾ oz/2 tablespoons unsalted butter
25 g/¾ oz/2 tablespoons plain flour
250 ml/8 fl oz milk
salt and freshly ground black pepper
freshly grated nutmeg
2 egg yolks
3 egg whites
120 g/4 oz blue cheese
75 g/2½ oz spring onions (scallions)

PASTRY
125 g/4⅓ oz/¾ cup plain flour
100 g/3½ oz/7 tablespoons unsalted butter, at room temperature
1 egg yolk
salt

F IRST make the pastry. In a food processor, combine the flour, butter, egg yolk, 2 pinches of salt and 1 tablespoon of water. Process for about 10 seconds or just until a dough is formed that clings to the blades, then turn out on to the work surface. With the palms of the hands, work the dough until it is smooth. Wrap the dough and chill for at least 30 minutes.

Meanwhile, cook the cauliflower florets in boiling salted water for about 15 minutes or until tender but not mushy (test with the point of a sharp knife). Drain in a colander and leave to cool.

In a small heavy saucepan, melt the butter until foaming, then add the flour and cook for 3 minutes, stirring constantly with a whisk. Pour in the cold milk and add 2 pinches of salt, and pepper and nutmeg to taste. Continue stirring with the whisk until the sauce boils, then lower the heat and leave the sauce to simmer gently for 15 minutes. Remove from the heat, add the egg yolks and mix very well. Cover the surface of the sauce with dampened greaseproof or parchment paper to prevent a skin forming, and set aside.

On a lightly floured surface, roll out the pastry dough to a round about 28 cm/11 inches in diameter. Use to line a 20–22 cm/8–8½ inch loose-bottomed tart tin, gently easing the dough in. Cut off the excess dough around the rim, leaving a 1.5 cm/scant ¾ inch overhang. Tuck this overhang under all around the rim so that the edge of the pastry case rises above the rim of the tin. Flute the edge and prick the bottom of the pastry case with a fork. Place in the refrigerator to rest for 15 minutes.

Preheat the oven to 190°C/375°F/gas mark 5. Place a baking sheet in the oven to heat.

BRUNO'S NOTES

This delicious, inexpensive dish can also be served as a light main course, with a mixed salad.

The best blue cheeses to use are Stilton, Roquefort or Gorgonzola, but not Danish blue cheese which is too sharp and salty.

Line the pastry case with greaseproof or parchment paper and fill it with baking beans. Place the tin on the baking sheet in the oven and bake for 10 minutes, then remove the paper and beans and bake for a further 5 minutes.

Meanwhile, in a large, clean stainless steel or glass bowl, whisk the egg whites with a tiny pinch of salt until firm but not too stiff: the mixture should hold its shape on the whisk when lifted out. Add to the sauce and fold in gently. (This operation is easy if you use a pastry scraper.) Crumble the cheese over the mixture. Add the cauliflower and chopped spring onions and mix together quickly and gently.

Pour the filling into the pastry case and level the top with the scraper. Bake for about 20 minutes or until the filling is just set and golden on the top. Serve immediately.

ENDIVES EN SURPRISE
Surprise Chicory

SERVES 4

150 g/5 oz smoked salmon
juice of ¼ lemon
cayenne or freshly ground white pepper
150 ml/5 fl oz whipping cream
4 heads of chicory (Belgian endive)
150 g/5 oz cucumber
salt
a bunch of fresh chives
a bunch of fresh dill (optional)
100 ml/3½ fl oz plain yogurt
½ teaspoon green peppercorns

PUT the smoked salmon in a food processor with 4 tablespoons of water and work to obtain a smooth consistency. Add the lemon juice and cayenne or pepper to taste. Whip the cream until stiff, then mix it with the smoked salmon purée. Put aside in the refrigerator for 5 minutes or so.

Separate the leaves individually from each head of chicory. Put some of the smoked salmon mousse in each leaf, then reshape the 4 chicory heads.

Peel the cucumber. Cut it lengthways into slices 3 mm/⅛ inch thick and then into very small dice. Spread the cucumber out on a plate, sprinkle with salt and leave to drain for 5 minutes. Then rinse the cucumber under cold running water and pat dry with paper towels.

Chop the chives and dill. Put most of the chives and all the dill in a small bowl and add the cucumber, yogurt and peppercorns crushed coarsely with the side of a knife. Stir to mix.

To serve, put a head of chicory in the centre of each plate, pour some spots of the yogurt dressing around and sprinkle over the remaining chives.

CONSOMMÉ DE CAILLES ET MIQUES AUX CÈPES

Quail Consommé Garnished with Cep Dumplings

SERVES 4

CONSOMMÉ
bones from 6 quails
(see recipe for Terrine de Caille aux Abricots Secs, page 48)
1 rasher of smoked streaky bacon (1 slice of country-style bacon)
100 g/3½ oz carrots
100 g/3½ oz onions
2 stalks of celery
150 g/5 oz white part of leeks
100 g/3½ oz tomatoes, preferably plum-type
2 cloves of garlic
2 tablespoons soy sauce
fresh chervil, to garnish

CLARIFICATION
1 skinless, boneless chicken breast (chicken breast half)
2 egg whites

MIQUES
10 g/⅓ oz dried ceps
2 prunes
1 rasher of smoked streaky bacon (1 slice of country-style bacon)
a small piece of garlic
60 g/2 oz bread
30 g/1 oz/3 tablespoons flour
2 pinches of baking powder
1 tablespoon mixed chopped fresh parsley and tarragon
1 egg
2 tablespoons milk
freshly grated nutmeg
salt and freshly ground black pepper

BRUNO'S NOTES

You can use chicken bones instead of quail bones. A dash of Sauternes will improve the consommé.

The clarification isn't as complicated as it may seem, and the result is a beautifully clear soup. Just be careful when ladling the consommé into the sieve that you don't break up the 'crust'.

If you do not have any dried ceps for the *miques*, you can use 100 g/3½ oz of fresh white mushrooms. Blanch them in the boiling consommé for 5 minutes to remove excess water, then drain and pat dry with paper towels.

PUT the quail bones and the rasher of bacon in a large pan and just cover with cold water. Bring to the boil quickly, boil for 1 minute and drain. Refresh under cold running water. (This blanching will clear impurities.)

Place the bones and bacon in a deep pan or stockpot. Peel the carrots and onions and cut into chunks. Cut the celery and leeks into chunks too. Add the prepared vegetables to the stockpot with all the remaining consommé ingredients and add fresh cold water to cover. Slowly bring to the boil, skimming any scum off the surface, then partially cover the pan and leave to simmer for 1 hour.

During this time, prepare the *miques*. Soak the ceps in warm water for

30 minutes, then rinse well to remove any hidden grit, and drain. Stone the prunes and chop coarsely. Remove the rind from the bacon, if necessary, and chop coarsely. Put the ceps, prunes and bacon in a food processor and add the garlic crushed with the side of a knife, together with all the other ingredients for the *miques*. Process until you obtain a coarse mixture that will bind together. Put this *farce* in the refrigerator to firm for at least 30 minutes.

Strain the soup through a fine sieve into a clean pan and bring back to a simmer.

Flour your hands and shape the *farce* into 1 cm/½ inch diameter balls. Add the balls to the simmering soup and cook for 20 minutes. Remove the *miques* with a slotted spoon to a shallow dish. Add a ladleful or two of the soup, and set aside in a warm place.

To clarify the consommé, put the chicken breast in the food processor with 4 tablespoons of cold water and process for 30 seconds. Turn into a bowl and add the egg whites. Mix very well, and add 4 crushed ice cubes. Bring the soup to the boil, pour in the chicken mixture and quickly mix with a large spoon. Reduce the heat to medium to bring the soup down to simmering point again and leave to cook for 15 minutes. During this time, the chicken mixture will form a sort of crust on the surface of the soup, and will collect all the impurities.

Ladle the consommé into a muslin- or cheesecloth-lined sieve placed over a clean pan, leaving the chicken and egg white 'crust' behind. When you can no longer ladle the consommé, carefully pour the remainder into the sieve. Discard the 'crust'.

To serve, reheat the consommé, put the *miques* in and ladle into 4 soup plates. Sprinkle some chervil on top to garnish.

SAUMON MARINÉ SUR L'ASSIETTE
Salmon Marinated on the Plate

SERVES 4

350 g/12 oz skinned salmon fillet
4 tablespoons olive oil
4 teaspoons Maldon sea salt
freshly ground black pepper
fresh mint and basil
juice of ½ lime

BRUNO'S NOTES

This is a very simple and refreshing first course. The herbs suggested here can be replaced by fresh coriander (cilantro) and dill, as you wish, and you can serve the salmon with a green salad and toast.

Because the salmon is not cooked, it is important to use only the very freshest fish.

S LICE the salmon fillet very finely using a very sharp knife. Arrange the slices side by side, not overlapping, on the plates to cover them. Brush the olive oil on the salmon, then sprinkle over the salt, a turn of the pepper mill for each plate, some chopped mint and basil and, finally, the lime juice. Serve immediately.

TATIN DE CÉLERI AUX TRUFFES DU PÉRIGORD
Celeriac Tart Tatin with Truffles

SERVES 4

1.4 kg/3 lb celeriac (celery root)
juice of ½ lemon
200 g/7 oz duck fat
200 ml/7 fl oz dry white wine
3 cloves of garlic
100 ml/3½ fl oz Jus de Veau (page 18) or duck stock
40 g/1⅓ oz truffles, fresh or canned
salt and freshly ground black pepper
Maldon sea salt

PASTRY
125 g/4⅓ oz/¾ cup flour
100 g/3½ oz/7 tablespoons unsalted butter, at room temperature
1 egg yolk
a pinch of salt

PEEL the celeriac and cut it in half. Cut each half into segments about 1 cm/½ inch wide, and trim the thin side of each segment to obtain a shape like that of an apple slice. Alternatively, cut the whole peeled celeriac into slices about 1 cm/½ inch thick; lay each round slice flat and cut it into small wedges like a pie. While the celeriac is being prepared, keep it in a bowl of cold water to which the lemon juice has been added; this will prevent the celeriac going brown.

Drop the celeriac segments into a pan of boiling salted water and blanch for 3 minutes; drain well.

Heat the duck fat in a pan, add the celeriac with the white wine and roughly chopped garlic and simmer for about 20 minutes or until the celeriac is soft.

Meanwhile, put all the ingredients for the pastry into a food processor and process for 10 seconds or just until a dough is formed that clings to the blades, then turn out on to the work surface. With the palms of your hands, work the dough until smooth. Wrap and leave to rest in the refrigerator for at least 30 minutes.

Bring the veal stock to the boil in a pan and reduce until nice and syrupy. Add the finely chopped truffles and put aside in a warm place.

Preheat the oven to 220°C/425°F/gas mark 7.

Drain the celeriac segments and use them to line four 10–12 cm/4–5 inch diameter tartlet moulds, arranging the celeriac segments side by side radiating from the centre. Season to taste.

On a floured work surface, roll out the dough to 3 mm/⅛ inch thick. Cut out 4 rounds slightly bigger than the tartlet moulds. Lay a round over each mould and, with the back of a knife blade, gently ease the edge of the dough

BRUNO'S NOTES

I created this dish in autumn, 1988, at the Inn on the Park when I first started working there.

The truffles can be replaced by chopped tarragon, but this will of course make a different dish. Also, you can use a mixture of 60 g/2 oz/4 tablespoons unsalted butter and 100 ml/3½ fl oz vegetable oil instead of duck fat.

You will have celeriac trimmings; use them in the Purée d'Hiver (page 118).

down between the celeriac and the mould. Make a small hole in the centre of each pastry lid so that the steam can escape during baking.

Set the moulds in a roasting tin containing a little water and bake in the hot oven for 10 minutes or until the pastry is golden brown and crisp.

Turn out the tarts, upside-down, on hot plates. Glaze the tops with the truffle sauce, sprinkle around some sea salt and pepper, and serve.

RILLETTES DE CRABE ET MORUE
Shredded Crab Meat and Salt Cod Bound with Curry Mayonnaise

SERVES 4

200 g/7 oz salt cod fillet
malt vinegar
200 g/7 oz white crab meat, preferably freshly cooked
4 spring onions (scallions)
3 tablespoons mayonnaise
mild curry powder
juice of ½ lemon
2 ripe avocados
fresh dill
¼ fresh coconut
4 tablespoons Vinaigrette (page 23)

BRUNO'S NOTES

You can use frozen or canned crab meat to make this dish, but freshly cooked crab is best as it will have the taste of the sea. To get 200 g/7 oz of white crab meat, you will need to cook 1 or 2 large live crabs (according to the type of crab): bring a pan of salted water to the boil with ½ wineglass of vinegar. Plunge the crabs into the water and simmer for 10 minutes. Remove from the heat and leave in the cooking water for a further 10 minutes, then lift out the crabs and set aside to cool completely. When cold, remove all the meat from the crabs. Any brown meat can be frozen and used in another dish.

THE day before, prepare the salt cod: put the fish in a basin of cold water to soak for 3 hours, changing the water every 30 minutes. When the water is changed, brush the cod gently with a stiff vegetable brush to loosen the salt. If the salt cod is very hard and dry, it will need to be soaked for a much longer time. After soaking, it should feel soft enough to squeeze between the fingers.

Put the cod in a pan of fresh cold water, add a dash of vinegar and bring to the boil. Boil for 10 minutes, then drain. Remove the skin and any bones and trim off any hard bits. Flake the flesh. Cover and keep in the refrigerator until ready to serve.

In a large bowl, combine the cod, crab meat, chopped spring onions, mayonnaise, 1 teaspoon curry powder and the lemon juice. Mix together with a fork.

With two large spoons, make a *quenelle* of the fish mixture in the centre of each plate. Cut the avocados in half, nick out the stones and peel them. Slice each half lengthways, not cutting all the way through at the narrow end. Gently open out the slices to resemble a fan. Place an avocado 'fan' on one side of each *quenelle*.

Sprinkle dill, a little bit of curry powder and the shredded meat from the coconut over the *quenelles*. Sprinkle the avocados with the vinaigrette. Serve immediately.

ASSIETTE DE FRUITS DE MER, PETITS LÉGUMES EN GELÉE, CRÈME D'ARTICHAUTS À L'HUILE D'OLIVE

Seafood Platter with Vegetable Aspic and an Artichoke Cream

SERVES 4

450 g/1 lb fresh cockles or small hardshell clams in shell
450 g/1 lb fresh mussels in shell
100 ml/3½ fl oz dry white wine
2 large scallops (sea scallops)
4 raw langoustines or king prawns (jumbo shrimp)
1 globe artichoke
juice of 1 lemon
salt
½ teaspoon Dijon mustard
about 100 ml/3½ fl oz olive oil
mixed salad leaves
4 spring onions (scallions)
60 g/2 oz white crab meat, preferably freshly cooked
½ tablespoon chopped fresh basil
½ tablespoon chopped fresh coriander (cilantro)
freshly ground black pepper

VEGETABLE ASPICS
300 ml/10 fl oz Fumet de Poisson (page 20)
1 egg white
½ leaf of gelatine
60 g/2 oz tomato, preferably plum-type
60 g/2 oz courgette (zucchini)
60 g/2 oz bulb of fennel
60 g/2 oz red sweet pepper

FIRST prepare the aspics. In a small saucepan, bring the fish stock to the boil. In a small bowl, beat the egg white with 1 tablespoon of water and 2 coarsely crushed ice cubes. Pour the egg white mixture into the boiling fish stock, give a stir and then reduce the heat to low. Leave to cook gently until the egg comes to the surface to form a skin.

Meanwhile, soak the ½ leaf of gelatine in a little cold water to soften it.

Strain the stock through a piece of muslin or cheesecloth stretched over a bowl or a muslin- or cheesecloth-lined sieve placed over a bowl. Squeeze the leaf of gelatine, add to the stock and stir until dissolved. Set aside.

Skin and seed the tomato and cut the flesh into 5 mm/¼ inch dice. Dice the courgette, fennel and red sweet pepper the same size. Plunge the sweet pepper and fennel dice into a pan of boiling salted water. After 2 minutes, add the courgette dice and cook for another 2 minutes. Drain in a colander and refresh in iced water. Pat dry with paper towels.

Mix all the diced vegetables with the fish stock and divide among 4 baba or other ring moulds, each about 8 cm/3¼ inches in diameter. Place these aspics in the refrigerator to set.

Scrub the cockles or clams and mussels thoroughly under cold running water. Place them in a small saucepan with the white wine, cover and cook over a high heat for about 5 minutes, shaking the pan occasionally, until the shells open (discard any that remain stubbornly closed). Drain in a colander placed over a bowl, to catch the juices. Pick the cockles or clams and mussels out of their shells and put aside in another bowl.

Cut the scallops into 1 cm/½ inch cubes. Pour the juices from the cockles and mussels back into the saucepan, add the scallops and cook for 1 minute. Remove the scallops with a slotted spoon and add to the cockles and mussels.

Twist off the heads from the langoustines. Cook the tails gently in the shellfish juices in the pan for 3 minutes. Remove the langoustines with a slotted spoon. Peel them and dice the flesh. Mix with the other shellfish, then pour over the shellfish juices. Set aside in the refrigerator.

Cut the stalk from the globe artichoke with a sharp knife. Starting from the base, cut off all the leaves by turning the artichoke around until you are left just with the artichoke bottom (*fond*). Put this into a small pan of water and add a squeeze of lemon juice and ½ teaspoon of salt. Cut out a round of greaseproof or parchment paper the same diameter as the saucepan and cut a steam hole in the centre of the paper. Place the paper round on the surface of the water. Bring to the boil, then reduce the heat and simmer for 25 minutes or until the artichoke is very soft (test it with the point of a sharp knife).

Drain the artichoke, reserving the cooking liquid, and cool it under cold running water, then remove the hairy choke with a teaspoon or your thumb. Slice the artichoke thinly and place in a blender with 2 tablespoons of the cooking liquid and the mustard. Blend briefly to mix, then with the motor running, slowly pour in 3½ tablespoons of olive oil. Set this artichoke *coulis* aside in the refrigerator.

To serve, unmould a vegetable aspic on the centre of each plate. Dress the salad leaves with a little olive oil and lemon juice, then put them into the centre of the aspic rings with the chopped spring onions. Arrange all the shellfish, including the crab meat, on the plates and sprinkle over the basil and coriander, a few drops of olive oil and a squeeze of lemon juice. Season with pepper. Surround with a ring of the artichoke *coulis*.

PIZZA DE CHAMPIGNONS
Mushroom Pizza

SERVES 4

250 g/9 oz puff pastry
20 g/⅔ oz/2 tablespoons shelled pistachios (optional)
30 g/1 oz/¼ cup shelled walnuts
30 g/1 oz/3 tablespoons blanched almonds
100 g/3½ oz shallots
400 g/14 oz mixed fresh wild mushrooms or open cultivated mushrooms
60 g/2 oz/4 tablespoons unsalted butter
1 clove of garlic
1 tablespoon mixed chopped fresh flat-leaf parsley and tarragon
salt and freshly ground black pepper
200 g/7 oz mozzarella cheese

O N a lightly floured surface, roll out the puff pastry to 3 mm/⅛ inch thick. Place it on a floured tray and chill in the refrigerator for about 20 minutes.

Meanwhile, if you are using pistachios, blanch them in boiling water for 3 minutes, drain and rinse under cold running water. Rub them gently in a linen towel to remove the skins.

Chop the pistachios, walnuts and almonds finely with a knife or put into the food processor for 10 seconds.

Peel and slice the shallots. Trim all the mushrooms, clean them thoroughly in cold water to remove all grit, and dry them well in a salad drainer. Cut them into pieces approximately all the same size. If using cultivated mushrooms, slice them.

In a frying pan, melt the butter over high heat and cook the mushrooms for 3 minutes, stirring frequently. Remove the mushrooms with a slotted spoon and drain in a colander. Add the shallots and garlic crushed with the side of a knife to the pan and cook in the mushroom liquid until the liquid has evaporated and the shallots are caramelised. Mix with the mushrooms, nuts, herbs, and salt and pepper to taste. Leave to cool on a plate.

Preheat the oven to 230°C/450°F/gas mark 8.

Take the puff pastry out of the refrigerator and cut it into four 15 cm/6 inch diameter rounds. With a knife, mark a ring inside each round, 5 mm/ ¼ inch in from the edge (this outside ring will rise during baking to make a rim). Place the pastry rounds on a lightly floured baking tray, and prick the centres of the rounds with a fork (don't prick the outside ring). Top with the mushroom mixture, spreading it out evenly but leaving the outside ring uncovered.

Bake the 'pizzas' for 8 minutes, then reduce the oven temperature to 180°C/350°F/gas mark 4 and bake for a further 4 minutes. Take the pizzas out of the oven, put some slices of mozzarella on each and bake for a further 3 minutes, to melt the cheese. Serve hot.

Filo pastry can be used instead of puff, if you prefer. Cut out four 23 cm/

BRUNO'S NOTES

This is a delicious and unusual alternative to the traditional pizza. It can also be made into 2 pizzas, to serve 2 as a light main course, in which case the cooking time should be increased a little. Serve with a chicory (Belgian endive) and bacon salad.

9 inch squares of filo for each pizza. Stack each set of 4 squares, first brushing each square with melted clarified butter or olive oil, and placing the squares on top of each other so that the points are in a different position each time. Then roughly fold over the points and sides into the centre several times to make a 1 cm/½ inch high rim on a round that is about 15 cm/6 inches in diameter. Top with the mushroom mixture and bake at 230°C/450°F/gas mark 8 for 7 minutes, then at 180°C/350°F/gas mark 4 with the cheese topping for 3 minutes.

SALADE DE M. VINICIO
Mr Vinicio's Salad

SERVES 4

1 red sweet pepper
1 yellow sweet pepper
5 tablespoons olive oil
1 very fresh bulb of fennel
250 g/9 oz ripe plum-type tomatoes
20 black olives
1 clove of garlic
1 tablespoon balsamic vinegar
salt and freshly ground black pepper
a large bunch of fresh basil
60 g/2 oz Parmesan cheese

BRUNO'S NOTES

Mr Vinicio is the restaurant manager at the Four Seasons Restaurant. He is a keen gardener and is very proud of the vegetables and herbs he grows. Being Italian, he has a special love for fennel, sweet peppers and tomatoes, so I have given this salad his name.

PREHEAT the oven to 200°C/400°F/gas mark 6.
Place the sweet peppers in a small heavy casserole or baking tin with 4 tablespoons of olive oil and 3½ tablespoons of water. Cover with foil, place in the hot oven and cook for 10 minutes.

Lift the peppers into a bowl and cover tightly (the steam trapped inside will help loosen the skin from the flesh). Leave to cool. Reserve the juices in the casserole.

Detach the large outside leaves from the fennel and put them aside for another use. Cut the heart into very fine strips and place in a large salad bowl. Slice the tomatoes and add to the fennel with the olives, the very finely chopped garlic, the vinegar and the remaining olive oil. Season to taste with salt and pepper.

Cut the peppers open, holding them over the casserole, and peel them with a small knife. Discard the core and seeds, and chop the flesh roughly. Mix with the other vegetables. Strain the juices from the casserole through a fine sieve over the vegetables.

Divide the vegetables among the plates. Chop the basil and sprinkle over the vegetables. Cut the Parmesan into fine shavings using a vegetable peeler and scatter over the top. Serve.

TERRINE DE CAILLES AUX ABRICOTS SECS
Quail Terrine Spiked with Dried Apricots

SERVES 10-12

6 oven-ready quails
celery salt
freshly ground black pepper
3½ tablespoons brandy
60 g/2 oz shallots
170 g/5½ oz/11 tablespoons unsalted butter, at room temperature
½ teaspoon fresh thyme leaves
2 cloves of garlic
100 ml/3½ fl oz Bristol Cream sherry
150 g/5 oz chicken livers
3 eggs
100 g/3½ oz/about ¾ cup dried apricot halves
250 g/9 oz unsmoked streaky bacon rashers
(slices of mild-cure bacon or salt pork)

BRUNO'S NOTES

When boning the quails, don't worry unduly about keeping them in one piece, nor about cutting through the skin. With the bones from the quails, you can make a consommé (see recipe on page 32). If, after marinating, the quails have not absorbed all the brandy, add any that remains to the liver mixture.

If you can make the terrine 2 days in advance of serving, it will taste even better.

BONE the quails, keeping the skin on. Arrange them on a tray, skin side down, and season with celery salt and pepper. Pour over the brandy. Cover and set aside to marinate in the refrigerator.

Peel and chop the shallots. In a frying pan, melt 20 g/⅔ oz/1½ tablespoons of the butter over low heat and add the shallots, thyme and the garlic crushed with the side of a knife. Sweat, covered, until the shallots are soft, without colouring. Pour in the sherry and boil, uncovered, for 3 minutes. Remove from the heat.

Trim any dark or discoloured bits from the chicken livers, then put them in a food processor with the remaining butter, melted. Process for 1 minute. Add the eggs and shallot mixture and season with celery salt and pepper. Process briefly to mix. Pass the mixture through a fine sieve into a bowl. Cover the bowl and put into the freezer for about 10 minutes to firm the mixture.

Meanwhile, put the apricots in a saucepan, cover with cold water and bring to the boil. Simmer for 5 minutes. Drain and cool under cold running water, then place the apricots on paper towels or a clean cloth to dry.

Preheat the oven to 150°C/300°F/gas mark 2.

Remove the rind from the bacon if necessary. Line a 25 × 8 cm/10 × 3½ inch terrine dish or loaf tin with the bacon, placing the rashers side by side and arranging them so that some hang well over the edge of the dish (they will be folded back over the top of the mixture, to cover it).

Start by putting a third of the liver mixture into the terrine. Cover with half of the apricots, then place 3 boned quails side by side on top. Repeat the layers, and finish with the last third of the liver mixture. Fold back the bacon rashers over the top. Cover with a doubled sheet of foil, and a lid if available.

Place the dish or tin in a deep roasting tin containing hot water. Cook in the oven for 40–45 minutes. To check if the pâté is cooked, insert a thin knife into the centre and leave it for 5 seconds; when withdrawn, it should feel hot and dry.

Remove the dish or tin from the tin of water and leave to cool at room temperature for 1 hour. Then cover closely and keep in the refrigerator for at least 12 hours before serving.

Serve in slices, with toasted country bread and Légumes au Vinaigre (page 148) or gherkins.

MOULES MARINIÈRES AU CRESSON
Steamed Mussels with Watercress Sauce

SERVES 4

1 kg/2¼ lb or more fresh mussels
Maldon sea salt
60 g/2 oz shallots
1 clove of garlic
a bunch of fresh parsley
150 ml/5 fl oz dry white wine
a bunch of watercress
100 ml/3½ fl oz double cream (heavy cream)
60 g/2 oz/4 tablespoons cold unsalted butter
¼ lemon
freshly ground black pepper

PREPARE the mussels by rubbing them with sea salt and then rinsing them under cold running water. Finally, put them in a large basin of cold water. Throw away all mussels that rise to the surface as they will be dead (mussels must always be cooked alive).

Peel the shallots and chop with the garlic and parsley. Put the mixture in a large saucepan, add the white wine and bring to the boil. Add the mussels. Cover the pan with a lid and cook for about 10 minutes or until all the mussels are open (discard any that remain closed after this time).

Meanwhile, pick the watercress leaves off the stalks.

Remove the mussels from their cooking liquor and keep them in a warm place. Strain the liquor through a very fine sieve into a clean saucepan, pressing down on the flavourings to extract all the liquid. Bring the liquor back to the boil, add the cream and boil again. Stir in the watercress leaves and boil for 4 minutes.

Turn down the heat to very low and whisk in the butter, in small pieces. Finally, add a squeeze of lemon juice.

Divide the mussels among hot soup plates and pour the sauce over. Grind some pepper over each plate and serve.

GROS RAVIOLES D'ESCARGOTS, SALADE DE COEURS DE LAITUE AUX LARDONS
Snail Ravioli with Lettuce and Bacon

SERVES 4

120 g/4 oz unsmoked streaky bacon (mild-cure bacon or salt pork)
75 g/2½ oz mushrooms
1 clove of garlic
1 tablespoon chopped fresh parsley
a slice of white bread
200 g/7 oz canned snails
30 g/1 oz/2 tablespoons unsalted butter
2 egg yolks
salt and freshly ground black pepper
250 g/9 oz Pâtes Fraîches (page 22)
½ teaspoon Dijon mustard
½ tablespoon white wine vinegar
½ tablespoon vegetable oil, plus a little extra for frying
4 'Little Gem' lettuces (or other small romaine-type lettuce)

BRUNO'S NOTES

This is a much more sophisticated way to eat snails than the traditional snails in shell with garlic and parsley butter. It will even appeal to people who are put off by the texture and aspect of snails.

REMOVE the rind from the bacon, if necessary. In a food processor, combine two-thirds of the bacon, the mushrooms, the garlic crushed with the side of a knife, the parsley and bread. Process for 2 minutes until you obtain a rough-textured *farce*.

Drain the snails and cut them into small pieces. Melt the butter in a sauté pan until foaming and add the snails and the *farce*. Cook for 10 minutes or until nearly all the juices have evaporated, stirring occasionally. Turn the mixture into a bowl. Add the egg yolks, salt and pepper, and mix very well.

Roll out the pasta dough on a lightly floured work surface with a rolling pin, or use a pasta machine, until the dough is 2 mm/scant ⅛ inch thick. With an 8 cm/3¼ inch pastry cutter, cut out 12 rounds.

Place a spoonful of the snail stuffing on each pasta round. With a wet pastry brush, slightly dampen the edges of the rounds, then fold them over to make half-moons and press the edges together to seal. Set the ravioli aside in a cool place until ready to cook.

In a large bowl, whisk together the mustard, vinegar and oil with 2 pinches of salt. Separate the lettuces into leaves, rinse in cold water and dry.

Cut the remaining bacon across into fine *lardons*. Heat a film of oil in a frying pan and sauté the bacon until crisp. Drain on paper towels.

While the bacon is being sautéed, cook the ravioli in boiling salted water for 4 minutes. Drain in a colander and rinse under hot running water. Tip the ravioli into a bowl, spoon over 1 tablespoon of the dressing and stir gently to mix. Put the lettuce into the large bowl with the remaining dressing and toss well.

Divide the ravioli among the plates. Put the dressed lettuce on one side, sprinkle over the bacon *lardons* and serve.

CAILLE RÔTIE EN SALADE
DE COLESLAW

Roasted Quails on a Coleslaw Salad

SERVES 4

4 tablespoons vegetable oil
4 oven-ready quails
1 curly endive (frisé)
1 tablespoon red wine vinegar

COLESLAW
2 egg yolks
1 teaspoon Dijon mustard
salt and freshly ground black pepper
150 ml/5 fl oz vegetable oil
90 g/3 oz carrots
90 g/3 oz white cabbage
1 Granny Smith apple
4 spring onions (scallions)
1 tablespoon red wine vinegar

PREHEAT the oven to 220°C/425°F/gas mark 7.
First make the coleslaw. Put the egg yolks in a bowl with the mustard and season with salt and pepper. Gradually pour in the oil, whisking constantly, to obtain a mayonnaise. Put aside.

Peel and grate or shred the carrots. Chop the cabbage very finely. Peel and core the apple and cut it into small strips. Chop the spring onions very finely. Mix these ingredients together with the mayonnaise and the vinegar. Set aside in the refrigerator.

Heat 2 tablespoons of oil in a sauté pan and seal and brown the quails on all sides. Turn them on to their backs and season with salt and pepper. Place in the hot oven and roast for 7–10 minutes. Remove the birds from the oven, lift on to a plate and leave to rest in a warm place for 5 minutes.

Meanwhile, trim and clean the curly endive. Dress it with the vinegar, the remaining 2 tablespoons oil, and salt and pepper to taste, and mix well.

Cut off the quail legs, then cut the breasts from the carcasses. Place the legs and breasts on a baking tray and reheat in the oven for 2 minutes.

To serve, place a good spoonful of the coleslaw on the middle of each plate, arrange the curly endive around, and place the quail pieces over the coleslaw.

TERRINE DE PETIT SALÉ, PURÉE DE POIS CASSÉS
Terrine of Pork Knuckle with Split Pea Purée

SERVES 10-12

2 kg/4½ lb salted pork knuckle (uncooked ham shank)
165 g/5½ oz carrots
165 g/5½ oz onions
4 stalks of celery
165 g/5½ oz leeks
1 bay leaf
2 cloves
8 black peppercorns
a bunch of fresh thyme
5 cloves of garlic
3½ tablespoons malt vinegar
350 g/12 oz/1¾ cups dried split peas
100 ml/3½ fl oz walnut oil
4 tablespoons tarragon vinegar
salt and freshly ground black pepper

SOAK the pork knuckle in cold water for 24 hours, changing the water every 6 hours; this will remove the excess salt.

Place the drained pork in a very large pot. Peel the carrots and onions and cut into big chunks; cut the celery and leeks into chunks. Add the vegetables to the pot with the bay leaf, cloves, peppercorns, thyme, garlic crushed with the side of a knife, and the malt vinegar. Add fresh cold water to come about 5 cm/2 inches above the level of the ingredients. Bring to the boil, then leave to simmer for 4 hours.

Remove the pot from the heat and set aside to cool until warm. Then lift out the pork. Remove the skin from the pork and reserve it. Take all the meat from the bones and trim the fat away with a knife. Drain the vegetables; reserve 200 g/7 oz and discard the remainder as well as all the flavourings. Cut the reserved vegetables into small pieces.

Line a 25 × 8 cm/10 × 3½ inch terrine or loaf tin with dampened grease-proof or parchment paper, and then with most of the skin of the knuckle. Fill with the meat alternating with the chopped vegetables. Finish with pork skin. Place a small wooden board on top of the mixture and put a heavy weight on the board to press it down. Refrigerate for at least 4 hours.

Meanwhile, put the split peas in a saucepan, cover with water to come 2 cm/¾ inch above the peas and bring to the boil. Cook gently for about 40 minutes or until tender. Drain the split peas in a colander and leave to cool. When cold, purée the split peas in a blender with the walnut oil and tarragon vinegar; season to taste with salt and pepper.

To serve, slice the terrine and put one slice on each plate. Brush the slices with walnut oil and sprinkle with pepper. Add a *quenelle* of split pea purée.

BRUNO'S NOTES

This terrine can be kept in the refrigerator, wrapped tightly, for a week.

At the Inn on the Park, I spike the terrine with some cooked foie gras, which gives a nice contrast of textures and richness.

If the pork cooking liquid is not too salty, it can be used as the base for a soup.

TERRINE DU PAUVRE
Smooth Pork Pâté

BRUNO'S NOTES

I call this dish Terrine du
Pauvre (Poor Man's Terrine)
because it's so cheap to make.

SERVES 10-12

50 g/1¾ oz canned anchovies
400 g/14 oz pork back fat (fresh fatback)
100 g/3½ oz onions
1 clove of garlic
1 teaspoon fresh thyme leaves
½ bay leaf
400 g/14 oz pig's liver
freshly ground black pepper
freshly grated nutmeg
thin slices of pork back fat (fresh fatback), to line dish

DRAIN the anchovies, rinse them in hot water and pat dry with paper towels. Set aside. Cut the back fat into large dice. Peel and slice the onions. Put the fat and onions in a saucepan and cover with cold water. Add the peeled garlic, thyme and bay leaf. Bring to the boil, then boil for 5 minutes. Drain in a sieve.

Turn the onion mixture into a food processor and add the anchovies and liver. Process until smooth. Season with pepper and nutmeg. Pass the mixture through a very fine sieve.

Preheat the oven to 180°C/350°F/gas mark 4.

Line a 25 × 8 cm/10 × 3½ inch aluminium terrine dish or loaf tin with the slices of back fat. Spoon in the liver mixture, spreading it evenly. Place the dish or tin in a roasting tin containing a little water. Cook in the moderate oven for about 1 hour. To test if the pâté is cooked, insert a thin knife into the centre and leave it for 5 seconds; when withdrawn, it should feel hot and dry.

Remove the dish or tin from the tin of water and leave to cool completely. When cold, cover and keep in the refrigerator for 24 hours before serving.

Serve sliced, with toast and chutney.

Rissoles de coquilles St Jacques à la 'chutney' de courgettes

Haddock en robe des champs

Pavé de saumon fumé à chaud, purée de pommes, jus de veau

Filets de truite aux condiments

Pavé de cabillaud, méli-mélo d'herbes et pommes nouvelles

Lasagne de cabillaud aux algues

Fricassée de saumon à l'étouffée de légumes et vinaigre balsamique

Aile de raie pochée, sauce tartare

Crépinette de barbue au chou, beurre de cidre

Solette rôtie à l'huile de crustacés et tomates confites

Filets de truite à la crème de kippers à l'oseille

Filet de carrelet à l'anglaise, sauce ravigote

Homard rôti à l'orange et cardamome

Maquereaux grillés, sauce verte

Ravioles de crabes à la citronelle

Tagliatelles de maquereaux à la tomate et aux câpres

Queue de lotte et coques à l'effilochée d'endives et laitue

Nage de coquilles St Jacques et bigorneaux à l'estragon et poivre vert

Merlan cuit en court-bouillon, sauce style rouille

Blanc de turbot braisé à la crème de pois frais au curry

CHAPTER THREE

Poissons

FISH

These days, a good choice of fish and shellfish is always available in fishmongers and many supermarkets. In this chapter, I use fish that are easy to find, as well as those which some chefs consider to be second rate. There are many theories about cooking fish, the most fashionable being that all fish should be steamed. I think there is a best way to cook every kind of fish. I would always braise or poach turbot rather than steaming it. I will never steam Dover sole, but will fry it *à la meunière*, with browned butter, lemon juice and parsley. I also try to get away from heavy cream sauces, which can be very good but which are used too often in fish recipes. For me, a simply cooked thick fillet of fresh cod (such as in the recipe here for Pavé de Cabillaud) or a grilled mackerel are hard to beat.

RISSOLES DE COQUILLES ST JACQUES À LA 'CHUTNEY' DE COURGETTES
Scallops in a Crisp Potato Shell, with a Courgette Chutney

SERVES 4

20 fresh scallops (sea scallops)
4 tablespoons olive oil
2 cloves of garlic
20 g/⅔ oz fresh root ginger
3 tablespoons soy sauce
salt and freshly ground black pepper
2 baking potatoes
cornflour (cornstarch)
oil for deep frying

COURGETTE CHUTNEY
150 g/5 oz onions
250 g/9 oz courgettes (zucchini)
olive oil
25 g/¾ oz/2½ tablespoons brown sugar
1 teaspoon tomato paste
1 clove of garlic
3½ tablespoons malt vinegar
1 tablespoon Worcestershire sauce

BRUNO'S NOTES

Under a crisp potato shell, a sweet, moist scallop with a sour-spicy chutney – one of the favourites at the Inn on the Park.

FIRST make the chutney: peel and finely chop the onions; cut the courgettes into very small dice. Heat a film of olive oil in a saucepan, add the onions and courgettes and cook for about 5 minutes. Stir in the sugar, tomato paste and garlic crushed with the side of a knife. Add the vinegar and Worcestershire sauce and stir to mix. Leave to cook gently for 20 minutes. When cooked, remove from the heat and set aside.

Remove the scallops from their shells, if necessary, and trim off any membrane, leaving just the white nut of meat. Cut the scallops in half if they are very large.

Mix together the olive oil, garlic crushed with the side of a knife, the peeled and chopped ginger, soy sauce, and pepper to taste in a bowl. Add the scallops to this marinade and refrigerate for at least 4 hours.

Peel the potatoes. Square off the sides, then cut into very thin slices – about 4 × 9 cm/1¾ × 3½ inches and 1 mm thick. You can cut the slices by hand using a very sharp thin-bladed knife, but a mandoline will make the job much easier. Dry the potato slices with a linen towel. Dip them into cornflour to coat on each side, then slap them with your hands to remove excess cornflour.

You will need 2 potato slices for each scallop. Place the slices on top of each other to form a cross and set the drained scallop in the centre. Fold over the ends of the potato slices to wrap the scallop completely like a parcel, and secure the parcel with wooden cocktail sticks.

Deep fry the parcels in oil heated to 180°C/350°F until golden and crisp on all sides. Drain on paper towels and season with salt.

Quickly reheat the courgette chutney. Put the scallops on hot plates with the chutney and serve immediately.

Suggested garnish: a simple green salad

Illustrated on PLATE 8

HADDOCK EN ROBE DES CHAMPS
Smoked Haddock in Jacket Potatoes
with Herb Butter

SERVES 4

4 large baking potatoes
500 g/1 lb 2 oz smoked haddock (finnan haddie)
200 ml/7 fl oz milk
100 g/3½ oz/7 tablespoons unsalted butter, at room temperature
1 tablespoon chopped fresh parsley
1 tablespoon chopped fresh basil
1 tablespoon chopped fresh tarragon
1 clove of garlic
freshly grated nutmeg
salt and freshly ground black pepper

BRUNO'S NOTES

You can replace the smoked haddock with fresh cod, if you prefer.

P REHEAT the oven to 190°C/375°F/gas mark 5.
Scrub and prick the potatoes. Bake them for 1¼–1½ hours or until tender.

Meanwhile, put the smoked haddock in a baking dish with the milk and cover with buttered greaseproof or parchment paper. Put into the oven to poach for 10 minutes. Drain the fish, reserving the milk, and flake the flesh, discarding all skin and bones. Set aside.

Mix the butter with all the herbs and the finely chopped garlic. Roll into a sausage shape, wrap and put into the refrigerator to firm.

When the potatoes are ready, cut a slice from the top of each and scoop out most of the insides with a spoon. Mash the scooped-out potato in a bowl with the milk reserved from poaching the fish, using a fork. Add nutmeg, salt and pepper to taste.

Fill the potato shells with the mashed potato and cover with the poached haddock flakes. Top each potato with a slice of herb butter. Set the potatoes in a gratin dish and heat in the oven for 10 minutes, then serve.

Suggested garnish: a large green salad

PAVÉ DE SAUMON FUMÉ À CHAUD, PURÉE DE POMMES, JUS DE VEAU
Hot Smoked Salmon with Mashed Potatoes and Veal Stock

SERVES 4

4 pieces of salmon fillet with the skin on, weighing 150 g/5 oz each
Maldon sea salt
1 kg/2¼ lb potatoes
200 ml/7 fl oz milk
100 g/3½ oz/7 tablespoons unsalted butter
freshly grated nutmeg
300 ml/10 fl oz Jus de Veau (page 18)
a small sprig of fresh rosemary
salt and freshly ground black pepper
vegetable oil

SPRINKLE the salmon pieces on both sides with 2 tablespoons of sea salt, and put aside in a cool place.

Preheat the oven to 180°C/350°F/gas mark 4.

Peel 800 g/1¾ lb of the potatoes and cut them into big chunks. Put them in a saucepan, cover with cold water and add a little salt. Bring to the boil and cook until soft – about 25 minutes depending on the quality of the potatoes.

When cooked, drain the potatoes in a colander and put them in a roasting tin, shaking the tin to spread the potatoes out evenly. Put into the oven for about 10 minutes to dry; this will give a better result with the mashed potatoes. Pass the potatoes through a mouli or potato ricer into a saucepan.

In a small pan, combine the milk, 45 g/1½ oz/3 tablespoons of the butter and nutmeg to taste. Bring to the boil, then pour over the potato purée and mix with a wooden spoon. Melt 30 g/1 oz/2 tablespoons of the remaining butter and pour over the mashed potatoes. Set aside.

Put some charcoal briquettes into a metal smoker and, if you can find them, add some vine cuttings or wood shavings from cherry, apple or plum trees. Place a grill over the charcoal and put the smoker over a high gas flame to heat until the charcoal starts to turn red and crack.

While the smoker is heating, put the veal stock into a saucepan with the rosemary and reduce to 200 ml/7 fl oz. Set aside.

Peel and finely grate the remaining potatoes, put them in a colander and rinse under cold running water. Drain and squeeze firmly in your hands to dry the potatoes as much as possible. Put them in a bowl and season with salt and pepper. Melt the remaining butter and mix it into the potatoes.

When the smoker is ready, put the salmon pieces on the grill, cover and reduce the heat underneath the smoker to low. Leave to cook for about 10 minutes or until the outside of the salmon is firm but the inside still moist.

Meanwhile, heat a film of oil in a non-stick frying pan. Place four egg poaching rings or muffin rings, each about 8 cm/3¼ inches in diameter, on

BRUNO'S NOTES

To obtain a richer mashed potato, you can add an egg yolk when reheating.

If you don't have a smoker, you can get a similar effect with a covered barbecue. Or the salmon steaks can simply be grilled, skin side down, on a barbecue.

the pan and spoon the grated potato mixture into the rings, spreading it out evenly to make galettes about 2mm/scant ⅛ inch thick. Remove the rings. Cook the galettes over a low heat until golden and crisp on each side. Put the galettes on a tray lined with paper towels and keep hot.

Reheat the mashed potato and stir well to mix in the butter. Spoon into a piping bag fitted with a large plain tube. Pipe the potato on to the centre of each hot plate to make a well, fill with the hot rosemary-infused veal stock and cover with a crispy potato galette. Remove the skin from the salmon, place it on the galettes and sprinkle round some sea salt and pepper.
Suggested garnish: a green salad

Illustrated on PLATE 9

FILETS DE TRUITE AUX CONDIMENTS
Trout Fillets Baked with Tomatoes, Ginger, Chilli and Lemon Grass

SERVES 4

skinned fillets from 4 trout
100 g/3½ oz tomatoes, preferably plum-type
60 g/2 oz shallots
1 clove of garlic
1 small green chilli pepper
1 stick of fresh lemon grass
1 teaspoon chopped fresh root ginger
saffron powder
24 capers
1 lime
salt
4 tablespoons virgin olive oil

PREHEAT the oven to 200°C/400°F/gas mark 6.
With tweezers, pick out all the bones from the fish fillets, then set the fish aside in the refrigerator.

Cut the tomatoes in half and discard the seeds, then cut the flesh into dice and put in a bowl. Peel and very finely chop the shallots and garlic. Very finely chop the chilli pepper and lemon grass. Add these to the bowl together with the ginger, a pinch of saffron and the chopped capers. Peel the lime, removing all the white pith, then cut into segments between the dividing membrane. Add the lime segments to the bowl. Mix all these ingredients well together.

Season the fish fillets with salt and place on an oiled baking tray. Top the fillets with the tomato mixture, and pour around a wineglass of water. Place in the oven and bake for about 10 minutes.

To serve, place 2 trout fillets on each hot plate and pour over a spoonful of the cooking juices and a tablespoon of olive oil.
Suggested garnish: 'Gabaldi' Provençale (page 105)

PAVÉ DE CABILLAUD, MÉLI-MÉLO D'HERBES ET POMMES NOUVELLES
Baked Cod Topped with a Herb and New Potato Salad

SERVES 4

10 new potatoes
olive oil
4 pieces of cod fillet, each about 2 cm/³/₄ inch thick
salt and freshly ground black pepper
a small bunch of fresh chervil
a small bunch of fresh dill
a small bunch of fresh tarragon
a small bunch of fresh parsley
a small bunch of fresh herb fennel
100 g/3½ oz fresh rocket (arugula) leaves
100 g/3½ oz celeriac (celery root)
2 shallots
1 hard-boiled egg
3 tablespoons soy sauce
1 tablespoon balsamic vinegar
3 tablespoons walnut oil

BRUNO'S NOTES

Choose thick cod fillet, cut from the centre – after cooking, it has a lovely flaky texture.

This dish does not really require a garnish. It's simple and light, based on the moist fish and the delicacy of the fresh herb salad.

PREHEAT the oven to 180°C/350°F/gas mark 4. Cook the potatoes in boiling salted water until tender.

Put a little olive oil into an ovenproof dish and place the pieces of cod fillet in it, skin side down. Season the fish with salt and pepper. Put the dish in the oven and cook for about 7 minutes or until the flesh of the cod is white but still moist. When ready, keep the fish warm until serving.

Meanwhile, prepare the herbs by taking the leaves off the stalks. Blanch the parsley in boiling water for 15 seconds; drain and refresh in iced water, then pat dry. Finely chop the rocket. Peel and slice the celeriac, then cut into fine *julienne*. Drain the potatoes and slice them. Peel and finely chop the shallots. Finely chop the hard-boiled egg. Mix all these ingredients in a bowl.

Combine the soy sauce, balsamic vinegar and walnut oil in a small saucepan and bring to a simmer over a very low heat. Pour over the salad ingredients and mix well.

Place a piece of cod fillet in the centre of each hot plate and spoon the vegetable salad over the top. Serve immediately.

LASAGNE DE CABILLAUD
AUX ALGUES

Lasagne of Fresh Cod in a Seaweed Sauce

SERVES 4

200 g/7 oz Pâtes Fraîches (page 22)
20 g/²⁄₃ oz dried seaweed (nori, wakame, or konbu)
¹⁄₃ cucumber
salt and freshly ground black pepper
vegetable oil
500 g/1 lb 2 oz fresh cod fillet
30 g/1 oz shallots
3¹⁄₂ tablespoons white wine vinegar
100 ml/3¹⁄₂ fl oz dry white wine
3¹⁄₂ tablespoons double cream (heavy cream)
100 g/3¹⁄₂ oz/7 tablespoons cold unsalted butter
a bunch of fresh dill
4 tablespoons soy sauce
juice of ¹⁄₄ lemon

ROLL out the pasta dough as thinly as possible using a pasta machine or a rolling pin. Cut out 12 rounds using a 12 cm/5 inch diameter pastry cutter. (Or cut the pasta dough into 12 cm/5 inch squares.) Cook the rounds in boiling salted water for 2 minutes, then drain and rinse under cold running water. Set the pasta rounds aside in a bowl of water.

Put the seaweed in a bowl of cold water and leave to soak for 15 minutes.

Peel the cucumber, cut it in half lengthways and remove the seeds with a teaspoon. Cut the halves across into 3 mm/¹⁄₈ inch thick slices. Mix the cucumber slices in a bowl with some salt, leave to drain for 5 minutes and then rinse with cold running water. Pat dry with paper towels and set aside. Drain the seaweed. If the pieces are large, cut them into strips. Set aside.

Heat a film of vegetable oil in a non-stick frying pan. Place the cod in the pan, skin side down, cover with a lid and cook over a medium heat for 10 minutes.

Meanwhile, peel and chop the shallots. Put them in a small saucepan with the vinegar and wine, bring to the boil and reduce until you have only 1 tablespoon of liquid left. Add the cream and bring back to the boil. Remove from the heat and whisk in the butter, in small pieces.

Pass the sauce through a very fine sieve into a clean saucepan, pressing down on the shallots to extract all the liquid. Mix in the seaweed, cucumber, chopped dill, soy sauce and lemon juice.

Skin the cod, flake the meat and stir into the sauce. Keep hot.

Reheat the pasta rounds in boiling water for 1 minute, then drain on paper towels. Place a pasta round in the centre of each hot plate and spoon over a little of the fish sauce. Repeat the layers, and finish with a pasta round. Season with pepper and serve immediately.

Illustrated on PLATE 6

FRICASSÉE DE SAUMON À L'ÉTOUFFÉE DE LÉGUMES ET VINAIGRE BALSAMIQUE

Salmon Braised on a Bed of Vegetables Flavoured with Balsamic Vinegar

SERVES 4

300 g/10 oz carrots
200 g/7 oz white part of leeks
100 g/3½ oz brown cap mushrooms
a bunch of spring onions (scallions)
300 g/10 oz chicory (Belgian endive)
¼ lemon
60 g/2 oz/4 tablespoons unsalted butter
1 clove of garlic
1 cardamom pod
curry powder
a small strip of orange zest
100 ml/3½ fl oz balsamic vinegar
salt and freshly ground black pepper
vegetable oil
4 salmon steaks, each weighing about 150 g/5 oz
1 green apple
1 teaspoon each chopped fresh tarragon and chopped fresh chives
2 teaspoons chopped fresh chervil

PEEL the carrots. Using the vegetable peeler, cut the carrots lengthways into shavings. Cut the leeks into *julienne*. Thinly slice the mushrooms and spring onions. Separate the chicory leaves, then blanch them in boiling water with a squeeze of lemon juice added for 5 minutes; drain.

Melt the butter in a flameproof casserole. Add the chicory, carrots and leeks and cook on a medium heat for about 5 minutes, stirring occasionally. Add the spring onions, mushrooms, finely chopped garlic, lightly crushed cardamom pod, 2 pinches of curry powder, the strip of orange zest and, finally, the balsamic vinegar. Stir to mix, and season with salt and pepper. Continue cooking for 10 minutes or until the vegetables start to become slightly sticky and shiny.

Meanwhile, heat a film of oil in a frying pan and fry the salmon steaks for 1 minute on each side to seal. Remove from the heat and set aside.

Peel and core the apple and cut it into thin slices.

Place the salmon steaks on top of the vegetables and sprinkle over the herbs. Add 4 tablespoons of water and the apple slices. Put a lid on the casserole and cook on a very low heat for 5 minutes.

To serve, spoon the vegetables and apple on to hot plates, place the salmon steaks on top and spoon over the sauce from the vegetables.

AILE DE RAIE POCHÉE, SAUCE TARTARE

Poached Skate Wings in a Parsley and Caper Sauce

BRUNO'S NOTES

If you wish, you can trim the fish from the bone after cooking it, but this will require more handling and the fish will cool.

SERVES 4

75 g/2½ oz shallots
4 skate wings, weighing in total about 1.5 kg/3½ lb
100 ml/3½ fl oz dry white wine
3½ tablespoons tarragon vinegar
salt and freshly ground black pepper
100 g/3½ oz tomatoes, preferably plum-type
25 g/¾ oz (about 2 small) gherkins or cornichons
100 ml/3½ fl oz olive oil
45 g/1½ oz/3 tablespoons unsalted butter
juice of ½ lemon
25 g/¾ oz/2 tablespoons capers
a few leaves of fresh flat-leaf parsley
1 tablespoon chopped fresh chives

PEEL and slice the shallots. Place them in a large saucepan, put the skate wings on top and add the white wine, vinegar and seasoning. Pour in enough cold water so that the liquid is level with the top of the fish. Bring to the boil, then cover the pan and cook on a medium heat for 10 minutes, depending on the thickness of the fish. (To test if the fish is cooked, cut into the thick part next to the bone: the flesh should no longer be pink.)

Meanwhile, skin, seed and dice the tomatoes. Dice or slice the gherkins.

Remove the fish from the pan and put it aside in a warm place. Strain the cooking juices through a very fine sieve into a measuring jug. Pour 100 ml/ 3½ fl oz of the juices into a blender and add the olive oil, butter and lemon juice. Blend for 2 minutes.

Pour this sauce into a small pan and add the capers, roughly torn parsley, chives, diced tomatoes and gherkins. Heat briefly, whisking constantly.

To serve, place a skate wing on the middle of each hot plate and pour the sauce over.

Suggested garnish: Spaghetti de Légumes (page 110)

Illustrated on PLATE 7

CRÉPINETTE DE BARBUE AU CHOU, BEURRE DE CIDRE

Diced Brill Wrapped in Parma Ham and Cabbage, in a Cider Butter Sauce

SERVES 4

100 g/3½ oz pig's caul
malt vinegar
400 g/14 oz skinned brill fillets
1 dessert apple
2 tablespoons chopped fresh parsley
salt and freshly ground black pepper
8 leaves of Savoy cabbage
4 thin slices of Parma ham
100 g/3½ oz shallots or onion
100 ml/3½ fl oz medium cider (hard cider)
2 tablespoons double cream (heavy cream)
125 g/4½ oz/1 stick cold unsalted butter
¼ lemon
paprika

BRUNO'S NOTES

The brill can be replaced by salmon or trout.

Don't worry about any holes in the caul because it is used just to provide a little fat and to protect the *crépinettes* during cooking. If you can't find pig's caul, you can wrap the fish and cabbage balls in muslin or cheesecloth, in which case you will have to steam the *crépinettes*, allowing 8–10 minutes.

PUT the caul in a bowl of cold water and add about ½ wineglass of malt vinegar. Leave to soak for 30 minutes.

Meanwhile, cut the brill fillets into 5 mm/¼ inch dice and put in a bowl. Peel, core and dice the apple the same size. Mix with the fish. Add the parsley and season to taste with salt and pepper. Set aside in the refrigerator.

Blanch the cabbage leaves in boiling salted water for 3 minutes; drain and refresh in iced water. Pat dry with paper towels.

Drain the caul, squeeze it dry in your hands and spread it out flat on the work surface. Cut it into 4 pieces.

Shape the fish mixture into 4 balls. Wrap each ball in 2 cabbage leaves and then in a slice of Parma ham. Finally, wrap in caul. Flatten each *crépinette* slightly and put into the refrigerator while you make the sauce.

Peel and finely chop the shallots or onion. Put in a small saucepan with the cider, bring to the boil and reduce by half. Add the cream and boil again, then whisk in the butter, in small pieces. Season with a squeeze of lemon juice. Remove the sauce from the heat and keep warm.

Cook the *crépinettes* in a frying pan over a low heat for 5 minutes on each side.

Put the *crépinettes* in the centre of hot plates and pour the cider butter sauce round. Sprinkle a little paprika over the sauce and serve.

Suggested garnish: Palets à l'Ail (page 119)

Queue de Lotte et Coques à l'Effilochée d'Endives et Laitue

Monkfish Braised in a Chicory and Lettuce Cream
(recipe page 72)

PLATE 5

Lasagne de Cabillaud aux Algues

———————

Lasagne of Fresh Cod in a Seaweed Sauce
(recipe page 61)

PLATE 6

Aile de Raie Pochée, Sauce Tartare

Poached Skate Wings in a Parsley and Caper Sauce
(recipe page 63)

PLATE 7

Rissoles de Coquilles St Jacques à la 'Chutney' de Courgettes

Scallops in a Crisp Potato Shell, with a Courgette Chutney
(recipe page 56)

PLATE 8

Pavé de Saumon Fumé à Chaud, Purée de Pommes, Jus de Veau

Hot Smoked Salmon with Mashed Potatoes and Veal Stock
(recipe page 58)

PLATE 9

Maquereaux Grillés, Sauce Verte

Grilled Mackerel with a Green Sauce
(recipe page 69)

PLATE 10

Filet de Carrelet à l'Anglaise, Sauce Ravigote

Fillet of Plaice Coated with Breadcrumbs
(recipe page 67)

PLATE 11

Nage de Coquilles St Jacques et Bigorneaux à l'Estragon et Poivre Vert

Scallops and Winkles in a Light Tarragon and Green Peppercorn Sauce
(recipe page 73)

PLATE 12

SOLETTE RÔTIE À L'HUILE DE CRUSTACÉS ET TOMATES CONFITES
Small Dover Sole Roasted with Shellfish Oil

SERVES 4

400 g/14 oz tomatoes, preferably plum-type
3½ tablespoons olive oil
a sprig of flat-leaf parsley
1 lime
4 Dover soles, weighing 350 g/12 oz each
100 g/3½ oz/⅔ cup flour
100 ml/3½ fl oz Huile de Crustacés (page 24)
45 g/1½ oz/¼ cup capers
1 tablespoon chopped fresh coriander (cilantro)
1 heaped teaspoon fresh thyme leaves and flowers
salt and freshly ground black pepper

PREHEAT the oven to 170°C/325°F/gas mark 3.
Blanch the tomatoes in boiling water for 10 seconds; drain and refresh in iced water, then skin them. Cut into quarters and remove the seeds, then cut the tomatoes into strips. Place them on a baking tray and sprinkle over the olive oil. Put in the oven to dry for 2 hours.

Meanwhile, blanch the parsley in boiling water for 15 seconds, refresh and dry well. Chop the parsley and set aside.

Peel the lime, removing all the white pith, and cut out the segments, cutting down on either side of the dividing membranes. Set the lime segments aside.

About 20 minutes before serving, heat a film of olive oil in a large non-stick frying pan. Dip the soles in the flour to coat them on both sides, and tap them with your hands to get rid of excess flour. Place them in the pan, two at a time, and fry to give them a nice golden colour on each side. As they are fried, put them on a buttered baking tray.

Bake the soles in the oven for 5 minutes or until the flesh is white but still moist: test by making a small incision along the backbone using a sharp knife. Trim off the brittle bones on the sides of the fish, and put the fish on hot plates.

In a sauté pan, slightly heat the shellfish oil. Add all the other ingredients, including the dried tomatoes, parsley and lime segments, and stir to mix. Spoon over the fish and serve immediately.

Suggested garnishes: Fenouil Braisé (page 116) and Palets à l'Ail (page 119)

FILETS DE TRUITE À LA CRÈME DE KIPPERS À L'OSEILLE

Steamed Trout Fillets in a Creamed Kipper and Sorrel Sauce

SERVES 4

fillets from 4 trout
200 g/7 oz tomatoes, preferably plum-type
3 shallots
100 ml/3½ fl oz dry white wine
1 kipper
100 ml/3½ fl oz double cream (heavy cream)
juice of 1 lemon
freshly ground black pepper
100 g/3½ oz sorrel leaves
1 tablespoon chopped fresh chives

WITH tweezers, pick out all the bones from the fish fillets, then set the fish aside in the refrigerator. Skin, seed and dice the tomatoes; set aside.

Peel and chop the shallots. Put them in a saucepan with the wine and bring to the boil. Boil for 2 minutes. Add the chopped kipper and cream and simmer for a further 5 minutes. Strain the sauce through a fine sieve into a small saucepan, pressing down on the kipper to extract all the liquid. Keep the sauce warm.

Take a sheet of foil and punch holes in it using the tip of a sharp knife. Lay the foil on the work surface and arrange the trout fillets on top, skin side up. Transfer the fish, on the foil, to a steamer. Sprinkle over lemon juice and pepper to taste. Cover and steam for 4 minutes.

Lift the foil out of the steamer, and remove the skin from the trout fillets. Arrange the fillets on hot plates.

Bring the sauce to the boil. Stir in the sorrel, roughly chopped, the chives, diced tomatoes and a squeeze of lemon juice. Pour the sauce over the fish, and serve.

Suggested garnish: Cannellonis d'Épinards et Artichauts (page 117) or simply boiled new potatoes

BRUNO'S NOTES

You can use salmon fillet instead of trout, but the steaming time will be longer as the fish is thicker.

FILET DE CARRELET À L'ANGLAISE, SAUCE RAVIGOTE

Fillet of Plaice Coated with Breadcrumbs

BRUNO'S NOTES

To my great desperation, one of the favourite dishes of my two little girls.

SERVES 4

flour
1 egg
salt and freshly ground black pepper
fine dry breadcrumbs
4 skinned plaice (flounder) fillets, weighing about 600 g/1¼ lb in total
vegetable oil

SAUCE RAVIGOTE
1 egg yolk
1 tablespoon Dijon mustard
salt and freshly ground black pepper
6 tablespoons vegetable oil
6 tablespoons olive oil
1 tablespoon chopped fresh parsley
1 tablespoon chopped fresh chervil
1 tablespoon chopped fresh tarragon
juice of ½ lemon
2 tablespoons very finely chopped shallot or onion

FIRST make the sauce: in a small bowl, combine the egg yolk, mustard, 2 pinches of salt and a pinch of pepper. Mix very well with a whisk, then start to pour in the two oils very slowly, whisking constantly. Keep whisking until you get a mayonnaise. Add the herbs, lemon juice, shallot or onion and 2 tablespoons of hot water and mix well. Set aside.

Prepare in front of you 4 plates: one with flour, one with the egg beaten with 2 tablespoons of water and a little salt and pepper, one with breadcrumbs, and one empty. Pass the fish fillets through the ingredient on each of the plates in the order given, to coat both sides, finishing on the empty plate.

Heat a film of oil in a large frying pan. Put in 2 of the fish fillets and cook for 5 minutes on each side or until a nice golden brown. Lift the fillets out of the pan and drain them on paper towels to absorb the maximum of fat. Keep hot while you fry the remaining fillets.

Arrange the fish fillets on hot plates with 2 *quenelles* of sauce on each side (you can make the shape of the *quenelles* with the help of 2 tablespoons). Serve hot.

Suggested garnishes: Pommes de Terre Frites (page 106), Maldon sea salt and a green salad

Illustrated on PLATE 11

HOMARD RÔTI À L'ORANGE ET CARDAMOME
Roast Lobster with Orange and Cardamom

SERVES 4

4 live lobsters, about 700 g/1½ lb each
olive oil
100 g/3½ oz carrots
½ bulb of fennel
1 leek (white part only)
150 g/5 oz tomatoes, preferably plum-type
a bunch of fresh thyme
a strip of orange zest
3½ tablespoons brandy
100 ml/3½ fl oz dry vermouth
1 clove of garlic
3 cardamom pods or ½ teaspoon ground cardamom
4 heads of chicory (Belgian endive)
juice of ½ lemon
60 g/2 oz/4 tablespoons cold unsalted butter
salt and freshly ground black pepper

BRUNO'S NOTES

The bitterness of the chicory, the sweetness of the lobster, and the deep flavour of the cardamom and orange all combine to give this simple dish a unique character. It can also be served as a first course, for 8.

BRING a large pot of water to the boil. In the meantime, put the lobsters into the freezer to make them sleepy. When the water is boiling, plunge the lobsters into it and boil for 3 minutes. Lift out the lobsters and put them into a basin of cold water (this helps to loosen the meat from the shell).

When cool enough to handle, twist off the legs and tails from the bodies. With scissors, cut open the underside of the tail and pull out the meat. With a hammer, crack the claws and extract the meat. Coarsely break up the shells; set the meat aside.

In a large saucepan, heat 100 ml/3½ fl oz of olive oil and add the lobster shells (reserve the ends of the tails and the heads for the garnish). Stir with a wooden spatula and cook the shells for 5 minutes.

Meanwhile, peel and finely chop the carrots; finely chop the fennel and white of leek. Cut the tomatoes in half and remove the seeds, then chop the tomato flesh; set aside. Remove the lobster shells from the pan using a slotted spoon and replace with the carrots, fennel, leeks, thyme and orange zest. Cook on a low heat until the vegetables are soft, without colouring, stirring frequently.

Put the lobster shells back into the pan. Add the brandy and warm it briefly, then set alight. When the flames die down, add the vermouth, chopped tomatoes, garlic crushed with the side of a knife and the cardamom (if using cardamom pods, crush them lightly). Stir well, then simmer for 20 minutes. Pass the sauce through a very fine sieve into a clean saucepan, pressing down on the shells and flavourings in the sieve to extract all the liquid. Set aside.

In a non-stick pan, heat a film of olive oil. Add the lobster meat from the bodies and 2 tablespoons of water and cook over a moderate heat, covered, for 5 minutes. Add the meat from the lobster claws and cook for a further 5 minutes, still covered.

While the lobster is cooking, separate the chicory into leaves.

With a slotted spoon, lift the lobster meat into a soup plate and add a squeeze of lemon juice. Keep warm. Put the chicory leaves into the non-stick pan with a squeeze of lemon juice and cook for 5 minutes or until tender, stirring occasionally.

Cut the lobster meat into big chunks and arrange on hot plates with the chicory leaves. Garnish with the lobster tails and heads. Bring the sauce to the boil and whisk in the butter, in small pieces. Season to taste. Pour the sauce over the lobster meat and serve.

Suggested garnish: Polenta Grillée (page 112)

MAQUEREAUX GRILLÉS, SAUCE VERTE
Grilled Mackerel with a Green Sauce

SERVES 4

4 large bay leaves
4 mackerel, weighing about 250–350 g/9–12 oz each, cleaned and gutted
100 g/3½ oz sorrel leaves
olive oil
Maldon sea salt
freshly ground black pepper
Sauce Verte Girondine (page 20)

CUT each bay leaf into 6 strips, on a slant, using scissors. With a very sharp knife, make 3 incisions on each side of each fish and put a piece of bay leaf in each incision. Chop the sorrel and put one-quarter inside each fish. Sew up the fish or skewer closed with wooden cocktail sticks. Turn the fish in a plate of olive oil to coat on all sides.

Wrap the tails of the mackerel in foil. Put the fish under a hot grill (broiler) and cook for about 8 minutes on each side or until the flesh is white but still moist: test by making a cut along the backbone with a sharp knife.

Transfer the fish to hot plates and sprinkle some sea salt and pepper over. Serve with the sauce verte.

Suggested garnishes: Canellonis d'Épinards et Artichauts (page 117) or boiled new potatoes and a green salad

BRUNO'S NOTES

When I was a boy in the South West of France, we often ate fish that had been grilled over a fire of vine cuttings.

Illustrated on PLATE 10

RAVIOLES DE CRABES À LA CITRONELLE

Crab Ravioli in a Lemon Grass Sauce

SERVES 4

a slice of white bread
1 egg
2 cloves of garlic
1 teaspoon chopped fresh coriander (cilantro)
1 teaspoon mild curry powder
250 g/9 oz freshly cooked white crab meat
60 g/2 oz freshly cooked brown crab meat
300 g/10 oz Pâtes Fraîches (page 22)
½ stick of lemon grass
4 tablespoons soy sauce
100 ml/3½ fl oz Huile de Crustacés (page 24)
juice of ½ lime
3 tablespoons olive oil

BRUNO'S NOTES

You can replace the bread with 4 large (sea) scallops, finely chopped; add the scallops with the crab meat.

Instead of pasta rounds, you can use wonton wrappers which can be bought in Chinese food shops. With wonton wrappers, the cooking time for the ravioli will be only 2–3 minutes.

PUT the bread, egg, 1 clove of garlic, the coriander and curry powder in a food processor and work until smooth. Turn the mixture into a bowl and mix in the white and brown crab meat. Cover and put into the refrigerator.

Roll out the pasta dough thinly using a pasta machine or a rolling pin, and cut out 32 rounds using a 6 cm/2½ inch diameter pastry cutter. With your fingers, stretch the rounds as thinly as possible without tearing them.

Place the rounds on a lightly floured work surface. Brush half the edge of one round with a little cold water, place 1 teaspoon of the crab mixture on one side of the round and fold it in two to make a half-moon shape, pressing the edges firmly together to seal them. Repeat until all the ravioli have been filled and shaped. Set aside.

In a small saucepan, combine 200 ml/7 fl oz of water with the chopped lemon grass and remaining clove of garlic, also chopped. Bring to the boil and boil for 5 minutes. Strain through a fine sieve into a clean pan, pressing down on the lemon grass to extract all the liquid. Add the soy sauce, shellfish oil and lime juice, and set aside.

Cook the ravioli in a large pan of boiling water for 5 minutes. Drain and rinse under hot running water, then return to the pan. Add the olive oil and gently toss the ravioli to coat them all evenly. Keep hot.

Briefly warm the lemon grass sauce, then mix it gently with the ravioli. Divide among the hot plates, and serve.

Suggested garnish: a salad of mixed leaves

TAGLIATELLES DE MAQUEREAUX À LA TOMATE ET AUX CÂPRES

Fresh Tagliatelle with a Tomato, Caper and Mackerel Sauce

SERVES 4

150 g/5 oz onions
300 g/10 oz ripe tomatoes, preferably plum-type
100 ml/3½ fl oz olive oil
1 tablespoon capers
60 g/2 oz (about 4 small) gherkins or cornichons
1 tablespoon chopped fresh parsley
3 cloves of garlic
500 g/1 lb 2 oz mackerel (cleaned weight)
1 tablespoon Dijon mustard
salt and freshly ground black pepper
3½ tablespoons dry white wine
300 g/10 oz fresh tagliatelle
60 g/2 oz Parmesan cheese

PREHEAT the oven to 180°C/350°F/gas mark 4.
Peel and chop the onions. Remove the seeds from the tomatoes, then chop them. In a saucepan, heat half of the olive oil, add the onions and cook gently for 2 minutes. Put in the tomatoes, capers, sliced gherkins, parsley and finely chopped garlic. Cook for 10 minutes, stirring occasionally.

In the meantime, place the mackerel on a large sheet of foil. Spread the mustard over the fish and season with salt and pepper. Add the wine. Close the foil tightly to make a parcel and place on a baking tray. Bake for about 10 minutes.

Open the foil and pour the juices into the tomato sauce. Flake all the flesh from the fish with the help of a fork, and discard all skin and bones. Add the fish to the tomato sauce. Leave to simmer very gently while you cook the pasta.

Bring a large pot of water to the boil and cook the fresh tagliatelle for about 3 minutes or until al dente. Drain in a colander and rinse under hot water, then tip into a bowl and add the remaining olive oil. Mix to coat all the strands of pasta with oil.

Divide the tagliatelle among hot plates, top with the mackerel sauce, and shave Parmesan over the top. Serve immediately.

QUEUE DE LOTTE ET COQUES À L'EFFILOCHÉE D'ENDIVES ET LAITUE

Monkfish Braised in a Chicory and Lettuce Cream

SERVES 4

400 g/14 oz monkfish tail
150 g/5 oz tomatoes, preferably plum-type
2 heads of chicory (Belgian endive)
1 soft-leaved lettuce
a few sprigs of fresh flat-leaf parsley
200 ml/7 fl oz dry white wine
100 ml/3½ fl oz double cream (heavy cream)
100 g/3½ oz/⅔ cup shelled freshly cooked cockles or small hardshell clams
60 g/2 oz/4 tablespoons cold unsalted butter
juice of ½ lemon
freshly ground black pepper

Remove any bone and membrane from the monkfish, then cut the fish into 2.5 cm/1 inch cubes.

Skin, seed and dice the tomatoes; set aside. Cut the core from the base of the chicory heads, then cut the chicory across into a fine *chiffonade*. Chop the lettuce roughly. Blanch the parsley in boiling water for 15 seconds; drain and refresh in iced water, then pat dry. Chop the parsley coarsely.

Put the monkfish cubes and white wine in a saucepan, cover with a lid and cook for 5 minutes on a low heat. Drain the fish, reserving the cooking liquor, and put aside. Pour the liquor into a clean pan and bring to the boil. Add the cream, chicory *chiffonade*, lettuce and cockles or clams. When simmering again, add the butter, cut into small pieces, the parsley, tomatoes and lemon juice. Stir well to mix. Season to taste with pepper – you should not need to add salt as the shellfish are very salty.

Put the monkfish cubes into the sauce to reheat briefly, then serve.
Suggested garnish: Pommes de Terre à l'Anis (page 107)

Illustrated on PLATE 5

NAGE DE COQUILLES ST JACQUES ET BIGORNEAUX À L'ESTRAGON ET POIVRE VERT

Scallops and Winkles in a Light Tarragon and Green Peppercorn Sauce

BRUNO'S NOTES

The success of this dish depends on the quality of the *nage*, which must be homemade.

The dish may also be served as a first course.

SERVES 4

2 litres/3½ pints/2 quarts fresh winkles (periwinkles)
10 black peppercorns
1 bay leaf
1 small green chilli pepper
Maldon sea salt
12 large scallops (sea scallops)
400 ml/14 fl oz Nage de Légumes (page 19)
12 green peppercorns
1 soft-leaved lettuce
2 tablespoons double cream (heavy cream)
100 g/3½ oz/7 tablespoons cold unsalted butter
a bunch of fresh tarragon
¼ lemon

RINSE the winkles in 4 or 5 changes of water until they are very clean. Put them in a large pot, cover with 5 cm/2 inches of water and add the black peppercorns, bay leaf, chilli pepper and some sea salt. Bring to the boil and simmer for 25 minutes, then drain in a colander. Pick the winkles out of their shells one by one using a cocktail stick, and cut the little black part off the end. Set aside.

Cut the scallops in half widthways.

Bring the nage to the boil in a large flat pan. Add the green peppercorns and the chopped lettuce. Put in the scallops and winkles and turn the heat to low. Add the cream and the butter, in small pieces, and move the pan so that the liquid swirls and incorporates the butter as it melts. Taste for seasoning and add the chopped tarragon and a squeeze of lemon juice.

Put the scallops and winkles in the middle of hot soup plates and ladle the liquid over. Serve immediately.

Suggested garnish: new potatoes

Illustrated on PLATE 12

MERLAN CUIT EN COURT-BOUILLON, SAUCE STYLE ROUILLE
Boiled Whiting Served with a Sweet Garlic Sauce

SERVES 4

1 onion
1 carrot
1 lemon
1 head of garlic
a bunch of fresh thyme
2 bay leaves
1 clove
a bunch of fresh parsley
1 egg yolk
1 hard-boiled egg yolk
1 teaspoon Dijon mustard
100 g/3½ oz/⅔ cup baked potato flesh
150 ml/5 fl oz olive oil
a pinch of saffron threads, soaked in 2 tablespoons hot water
Tabasco sauce
salt
4 whiting, weighing about 200 g/7 oz each, cleaned

BRUNO'S NOTES

Fresh cod steaks will do here, too, but whiting is the best fish for this recipe.

PEEL and thinly slice the onion and carrot; slice half the lemon. Put the onion, carrot, lemon slices, 3 peeled cloves of garlic, the thyme, bay leaves, clove and parsley in a saucepan. Cover with 1 litre/1¾ pints/1 quart of cold water and bring to the boil. Leave this court-bouillon to simmer for 15 minutes.

Meanwhile, peel the remaining garlic cloves and cook in boiling water until they are tender: test by squeezing a clove between your fingers. Drain the garlic in a colander and cool under cold running water.

In a food processor, combine the garlic, raw and hard-boiled egg yolks, mustard and baked potato flesh and work until smooth. Slowly pour in the olive oil, with the motor running, to make a mayonnaise consistency. Add the juice from the remaining lemon half, the saffron, and Tabasco and salt to taste. Set aside.

Put the whiting into the gently simmering court-bouillon to cook for 10 minutes.

Scoop out 100 ml/3½ fl oz of the court-bouillon and strain it into a small saucepan. Bring to the boil and whisk in the garlic mayonnaise.

Lift the fish out of the court-bouillon and drain on paper towels. Cover each plate with some garlic sauce, put a fish on top and serve.

Suggested garnish: Ratatouille (page 111) or Pommes de Terre à l'Anis (page 107)

BLANC DE TURBOT BRAISÉ À LA CRÈME DE POIS FRAIS AU CURRY

Turbot Braised with a Curried Cream of Fresh Peas

SERVES 4

75 g/2½ oz shallots
60 g/2 oz white button mushrooms
60 g/2 oz/4 tablespoons unsalted butter
100 ml/3½ fl oz dry vermouth
600 g/1¼ lb skinned turbot fillets
a bunch of spring onions (scallions)
a few sprigs of fresh parsley
200 g/7 oz/1⅓ cups shelled fresh peas
100 ml/3½ fl oz double cream (heavy cream)
½ tablespoon finely chopped fresh thyme leaves
1 tablespoon chopped fresh chives
½ teaspoon mild curry powder
¼ lemon
salt

BRUNO'S NOTES

Brill or Dover sole fillets can be used instead of turbot. You can also replace the fresh peas with frozen ones, cooked according to packet directions.

Preheat the oven to 180°C/350°F/gas mark 4.
    Peel and slice the shallots; trim and slice the mushrooms. In a wide flameproof baking dish, sweat the shallots in half of the butter on a low heat, covered, until soft, without colouring. Add the sliced mushrooms and pour in the vermouth. Bring to the boil. Arrange the fish fillets in this *braisage* and cover with buttered foil or greaseproof or parchment paper. Place in the oven to cook for 12 minutes.

Meanwhile, trim the spring onions and cut them on a slant into 2.5 cm/ 1 inch pieces. Blanch in boiling water for 1 minute; drain and refresh in iced water. Blanch the parsley for 15 seconds, refresh and pat dry, then chop coarsely. Cook the peas for 4 minutes; drain and refresh.

Remove the fish from the baking dish, cover and keep in a warm place. Strain the *braisage* through a fine sieve into a clean medium-sized saucepan, pressing down on the flavourings in the sieve to extract all their liquid. Bring to the boil, then stir in the cream, peas and spring onions. When the sauce comes back to simmering point, add all the herbs and the remaining butter, cut into small pieces. Mix with a wooden spoon to incorporate the butter. Season with the curry powder, a squeeze of lemon juice and salt to taste.

Place the fish in the centre of hot plates, pour the sauce over and serve.
Suggested garnish: Pommes de Terre à l'Anis (page 107) or simply boiled new potatoes

Carré d'agneau en croûte d'herbes au curcuma

Fricassée de rognons de veau au vin piqué

Filet de chevreuil dans une sauce réglisse et vin rouge

Longe de porc en cocotte à la vanille

Queue de boeuf mijotée aux pruneaux et au vinaigre

Sauté de cous d'agneau à l'orange

Râble et cuisse de lapin aux tomates douces

Volaille à l'indienne

Confit de canard au vin aux figues

Souris d'agneau aux flageolets et persil plat

Parmentier de canard

Escalope de foie de veau Mauricette

Pigeon des bois en jambon dans sa sauce à l'hydromel

Contre-filet de boeuf grillé, confit d'échalottes aux graines de moutarde

Caille rôtie, purée de pommes de terre à l'huile de noix

Poule au pot 'Henri IV', sauce verte

Jarret de veau mijoté à la sauge et à l'orange

Poulet des landes rôti à l'ail et au citron

Tétras rôties, salade tiède de navets

Pintade rôtie au céleri et ses tartines

Faisan rôti à la choucroûte fraîche, son jus à l'abricot

CHAPTER FOUR

Viandes

MEAT

I must say, the best lamb and beef I have ever tasted is British, which must prove that Great Britain has some very superior products. The quality of the meat in supermarkets is quite good, the only problem being that sometimes it is not cut as it should be. When shopping, I suggest you choose free-range poultry, and do not hesitate to try birds such as wood pigeon or unusual cuts of meat like neck of lamb and veal knuckle. Offal is also good value, and can be very tasty. In preparing the recipes here, I have tried to keep the dishes as simple as possible without too many stocks or unnecessary garnishes on the plate – just the main ingredients cooked in a special way, and lifted with a sauce.

CARRÉ D'AGNEAU EN CROÛTE D'HERBES AU CURCUMA
Roast Rack of Lamb with a Turmeric and Herb Crumble

SERVES 4

2 racks of lamb from best end, each with 6 bones, chined
3½ tablespoons olive oil
salt and freshly ground black pepper
100 g/3½ oz shallots
100 g/3½ oz canned Italian tomatoes (drained weight)
2 cloves of garlic
a bunch of fresh thyme
100 ml/3½ fl oz dry white wine
100 ml/3½ fl oz Jus de Veau (page 18) or 4 tablespoons soy sauce mixed
with 100 ml/3½ fl oz water
2 slices of white bread
1 tablespoon chopped fresh parsley
1 teaspoon dried herbes de Provence
½ teaspoon turmeric
2 tablespoons Meaux mustard

BRUNO'S NOTES

We are very lucky in England to have a constantly high quality of lamb available all year round.

PREHEAT the oven to 200°C/400°F/gas mark 6.
Trim most of the fat from the racks of lamb, leaving a thin layer. Scrape off all the meat and sinews from the ends of the bones.

Heat a film of olive oil in a roasting tin on top of the stove and seal the racks of lamb on all sides. Season the lamb with salt and pepper, then place it in the hot oven and roast for 8 minutes. Turn the racks over and roast for another 8 minutes.

Meanwhile, peel and chop the shallots. Chop the tomatoes.

Remove the racks of lamb from the oven and leave to rest on a wire rack placed over a dish in a warm place for about 10 minutes.

Pour off all but 2 tablespoons of fat from the roasting tin. Add the shallots to the tin and cook over a moderate heat on top of the stove for 2 minutes. Add the tomatoes, 1 clove of garlic crushed with the side of a knife, the thyme and the white wine and stir well. Bring to the boil and simmer for 5 minutes, stirring occasionally. Stir in the veal stock and simmer for another 5 minutes. Strain through a very fine sieve or muslin or cheesecloth into a saucepan and put aside.

While the sauce is simmering, combine the bread, remaining clove of garlic, the parsley, herbes de Provence and turmeric in a food processor and process for 1 minute or until fine and evenly coloured. Heat 2 tablespoons of olive oil in a frying pan, add the bread mixture and cook over a low heat for 5 minutes, stirring with a wooden spoon, until you obtain a nice crumble that will stick together a bit. Be careful not to let it brown. Turn on to a plate.

Trim all the fat from the racks of lamb. Spread the mustard over the meaty side, then coat them in the crumble, pressing with your hands to make it stick well. Place the racks under a hot grill (broiler) until the crumble topping is nice and golden.

Meanwhile, reheat the sauce.

To serve, carefully carve the racks between the bones, place on hot plates and spoon the sauce around.

Suggested garnishes: Petites Moussakas (page 102) and some plainly cooked new vegetables

FRICASSÉE DE ROGNONS DE VEAU AU VIN PIQUÉ
Sautéed Veal Kidney in Sour Wine Sauce

SERVES 4

700 g/1½ lb veal kidney (cleaned weight)
100 g/3½ oz shallots
5 juniper berries
2 tablespoons vegetable oil
30 g/1 oz/2 tablespoons unsalted butter
1 clove of garlic
¼ bay leaf
4 tablespoons gin
100 ml/3½ fl oz sour red wine
100 ml/3½ fl oz Jus de Veau (page 18)
salt and freshly ground black pepper

BRUNO'S NOTES

If you have any wine left over after a party, keep it in an open jar in your kitchen for a week and it will become sour. Sour wine is excellent for cooking as you get all the flavours and characteristics of the wine as well as those of a good old vinegar. I particularly like to use sour wine when cooking offal.

CUT the veal kidney into 2 cm/¾ inch pieces, discarding the core. Peel the shallots and chop very finely. Heat the juniper berries in a small frying pan until they smell aromatic; set aside.

Heat the oil in a sauté pan until very hot, add the pieces of kidney and sauté for 2 minutes, stirring with a wooden spoon to cook evenly. Tip into a sieve placed over a bowl to drain. Set aside in a warm place.

In the same pan, melt the butter and add the shallots, garlic crushed with the side of a knife, the bay leaf and juniper berries. Cook for 2 minutes, then stir in the gin followed by the wine. Boil to reduce until you have only 3 tablespoons of liquid left. Add the veal stock and reduce for a further 5 minutes.

Add the juices from the kidneys. Strain the sauce through a very fine sieve into a clean pan, pressing down on the vegetables and flavourings to extract all the liquid. Add salt and pepper to taste.

Put the pieces of kidney into the sauce and reheat for 2 minutes, then serve.

Suggested garnish: Macaronis Farcis (page 109)

FILET DE CHEVREUIL DANS UNE SAUCE RÉGLISSE ET VIN ROUGE

Roast Fillet of Venison in a Liquorice-Flavoured Red Wine Sauce

SERVES 4

750 g/1 lb 10 oz piece of fillet (tenderloin) of venison
1 teaspoon juniper berries
60 g/2 oz shallots
100 g/3½ oz celeriac (celery root)
60 g/2 oz carrots
60 g/2 oz mushrooms
olive oil
a bunch of fresh thyme
1 bay leaf
2 cloves of garlic
pared zest of ½ orange
3½ tablespoons red wine vinegar
500 ml/16 fl oz full-bodied red wine
2 tablespoons dark treacle or molasses
5 tablespoons soy sauce
1½ tablespoons gin
150 g/5 oz cooked beetroot (beet)
a small piece of cold unsalted butter
freshly ground black pepper

BRUNO'S NOTES

For the sauce it is important to use a rich, strong red wine such as Madiran or a North African wine.

Venison can be replaced by lamb fillet, in which case marinate in the wine for 12 hours before cooking. (American cooks can substitute a boneless loin of lamb cut from a rack of lamb.)

TRIM the membrane and nerves from the venison and reserve. Set the meat aside in a cool place.

In a small pan, heat the juniper berries for 2 minutes (this will intensify the flavour); set aside. Peel and finely chop the shallots. Peel and dice the celeriac and carrots; dice the mushrooms.

Heat a film of olive oil in a saucepan and add the venison trimmings, the shallots, celeriac, mushrooms and carrots. Cook, stirring occasionally, until nicely golden. Add the juniper berries, thyme, bay leaf, garlic crushed with the side of a knife, and the orange zest. Deglaze the pan with the red wine vinegar, stirring well, then add the red wine and bring to the boil. Reduce by half.

Stir in the treacle or molasses, 200 ml/7 fl oz of water and the soy sauce. Leave to simmer for 1 hour or until reduced to a shiny sauce-like consistency. The dark treacle in the sauce gives it a liquorice flavour.

About 20 minutes before the sauce has finished reducing, cook the venison: heat a film of olive oil in an oval flameproof casserole and seal the meat on all sides. Reduce the heat, put the lid on the casserole and cook for about 10 minutes. Turn the venison with a spoon twice during the cooking.

Uncover the casserole, add the gin and warm it briefly, then set alight. When the flames die down, remove the venison to a rack and set aside in a warm place to rest for 5 minutes. Add the juices to the sauce.

Meanwhile, peel and dice the beetroot.

Strain the sauce through a fine sieve into a clean saucepan, pressing down on the vegetables and flavourings to extract all the liquid. Bring the sauce to the boil. Whisk in the butter, then season with pepper to taste. Add the beetroot.

Slice the venison as thick as you like, arrange on hot plates and pour the sauce over. Serve immediately.

Suggested garnish: Purée d'Hiver (page 118)

Illustrated on PLATE 14

LONGE DE PORC EN COCOTTE À LA VANILLE
Loin of Pork 'Pot-Roasted' with Vanilla

SERVES 4

1 boned loin of pork, weighing about 600 g/1¼ lb, rolled and tied
1 vanilla pod (vanilla bean)
2 cloves of garlic
salt and freshly ground black pepper
vegetable oil
6 tablespoons rice vinegar or white wine vinegar
2 tablespoons white rum
250 ml/8 fl oz canned unsweetened coconut milk

BRUNO'S NOTES

This is an exotic way to prepare pork. The dish does not need a sauce because the meat is so moist.

You can buy cans of coconut milk in Indian shops.

P REHEAT the oven to 180°C/350°F/gas mark 4.
With the tip of a very sharp knife, make some incisions in the skin of the pork loin. Into each cut, put a piece of vanilla pod and a thin slice of garlic dipped in salt and pepper.

Put a film of oil in a heavy flameproof casserole that is just big enough to hold the pork. Heat the oil and seal the pork all over. Turn the pork skin side up and put the lid on the casserole. Place in the oven to cook for about 20 minutes.

Pour off all the fat from the casserole. Deglaze the pot with the vinegar and rum, stirring well, then put the casserole over the heat on top of the stove and reduce for 2 minutes. Stir in the coconut milk. Put back into the oven, without the lid, and cook for a further 15 minutes or until the pork is tender and cooked through.

Lift the pork on to a rack and leave to rest in a warm place for 10 minutes, then slice and serve.

Suggested garnishes: boiled rice and Oignons au Four au Gingembre (page 116)

Illustrated on PLATE 16

QUEUE DE BOEUF MIJOTÉE AUX PRUNEAUX ET AU VINAIGRE
Braised Oxtail with Prunes and Vinegar

SERVES 4

1 oxtail, weighing, about 1.2 kg/2½ lb
2 onions
200 g/7 oz carrots
4 stalks of celery
300 g/10 oz leeks
vegetable oil
30 g/1 oz/2 tablespoons unsalted butter
90 g/3 oz button mushrooms
4 tablespoons red wine vinegar
100 ml/3½ fl oz Jus de Veau (page 18)
a strip of orange zest
3 cloves of garlic
1 bouquet garni
1 tablespoon Worcestershire sauce
salt and freshly ground black pepper
150 g/5 oz stoned prunes

CHOP the oxtail into chunks or have the butcher do this for you. Peel and quarter the onions. Peel and thinly slice the carrots. Cut the celery into 3 cm/1¼ inch chunks. Trim the leeks and cut into 3 cm/1¼ inch pieces.

Heat a thin film of oil in a large saucepan over high heat. Add the oxtail chunks, a few at at time, and seal and brown on all sides. Transfer to a plate.

In the same pan, melt the butter over a low heat and cook all the prepared vegetables and the mushrooms for 15 minutes or until they are nice and golden, stirring occasionally. Deglaze the pan with the vinegar, stirring well, then add the veal stock, orange zest, garlic crushed with the side of a knife, the bouquet garni, Worcestershire sauce and 500 ml/16 fl oz of water. Season to taste with salt and pepper. Bring to the boil.

Return the oxtail to the pan, and leave to simmer gently for 2½ hours. During the cooking, skim the surface of the liquid from time to time to remove all the fat.

Remove the oxtail and put to one side. Strain the cooking liquid through a fine sieve into a clean pan, pressing down on the vegetables and flavourings to extract all their liquid. Add the prunes to the cooking liquid. Bring to the boil and reduce to a shiny, sauce-like consistency.

To serve, divide the oxtail among hot soup plates and spoon the sauce over. Alternatively, you can serve the oxtail with all the cooking vegetables in the sauce.

Suggested garnish: Purée d'Hiver (page 118) or Petits Choux Farcis Grand-Mère (page 104)

Illustrated on PLATE 15

SAUTÉ DE COUS D'AGNEAU À L'ORANGE
Sauté of Neck of Lamb with Orange

BRUNO'S NOTES

I think the fillet from the middle neck of lamb is better than that from the best end because it is more tender and has more flavour. It is also cheaper. There is no exact equivalent American cut for lamb fillet, but American cooks can use 2 boneless loins of lamb cut from the rack of lamb, shoulder end.

If you prefer your lamb cooked medium, allow 2 minutes for the initial sautéing.

SERVES 4

4 fillets of lamb, taken from the middle neck (see note)
salt and freshly ground black pepper
3 carrots
1 onion
2 large turnips
4 stalks of celery
1 orange
olive oil
½ tablespoon tomato paste
2 cloves of garlic
a branch of fresh thyme or 2 pinches of dried thyme
½ wineglass of dry white wine (optional)
4 tablespoons soy sauce
powdered saffron
chopped fresh parsley and basil (optional)

CUT the fillets across into medallions, each about 1 cm/½ inch thick – you will probably get 6 medallions from each fillet, depending on its length. Season the medallions with salt and pepper.

Peel the carrots, onion and turnips; cut them into small dice. Dice the celery too. Pare the zest from the orange and cut it into fine *julienne*.

Heat a film of olive oil in a sauté pan. Add the lamb medallions and sauté for about 1 minute to seal and brown on both sides. Transfer them to a colander placed in a bowl to drain (the juices from the meat will be incorporated into the sauce later).

In the same pan, heat a little more oil and add all the diced vegetables. Cook over a low heat until golden, stirring occasionally. Add the tomato paste, finely chopped garlic, thyme and orange zest. Deglaze the pan with the white wine, if you are using it, and bring to the boil, stirring well. Add the juice from the orange, the soy sauce, a pinch of saffron and the juices drained from the meat. Leave to simmer for 5 minutes.

Put the lamb medallions into the sauce to reheat for about 30 seconds. Add pepper to taste, with some chopped parsley and basil if you like.

Arrange the medallions on hot plates and spoon the sauce over. Serve immediately.

Suggested garnish: fine green beans or mange-tout (snow peas)

RÂBLE ET CUISSE DE LAPIN AUX TOMATES DOUCES

Roasted Saddle and Leg of Rabbit with Sun-Dried Tomatoes and Parma Ham

SERVES 4

2 saddles of rabbit (complete with bones and liver)
4 legs of rabbit
salt
1 teaspoon dried green peppercorns
100 g/3½ oz Tomates Douces Sechées au 'Soleil' (page 150)
6–8 thin slices of Parma ham

SAUCE
100 g/3½ oz carrots
100 g/3½ oz onion
60 g/2 oz celery
100 g/3½ oz white button mushrooms
four for coating
vegetable oil
1 clove of garlic
2 tablespoons light soy sauce
100 ml/3½ fl oz dry white wine
a sprig of fresh parsley
45 g/1½ oz/3 tablespoons cold unsalted butter
tarragon vinegar
freshly ground black pepper

BRUNO'S NOTES

If you are using sun-dried tomatoes in packets, they should be soaked in warm water until they soften, then drained and dried.

ASK your butcher to bone the saddles of rabbit and to keep the bones and liver.

First make the sauce: peel the carrots and onion; dice all the vegetables. Lightly flour the bones from the saddles and the rabbit legs. Heat a film of oil in a saucepan over high heat, add the bones, legs and diced vegetables and cook briskly until nicely golden brown, stirring occasionally. Add the garlic crushed with the side of a knife, the soy sauce, white wine and enough water to cover the ingredients. Bring to the boil and simmer for 35 minutes.

Meanwhile, heat a film of oil in a small frying pan and fry the rabbit liver to brown and seal it well on both sides. It should still be pink in the centre. Set aside.

Drop the parsley for the sauce into boiling water and blanch for 15 seconds, then drain and refresh in iced water. Pat dry and chop the parsley roughly. Set aside.

Preheat the oven to 200°C/400°F/gas mark 6.

Season the saddles of rabbit with a pinch of salt and sprinkle over the coarsely crushed green peppercorns. Rinse the dried tomatoes to remove any oil and pat dry with paper towels, then arrange in the fold of the saddles and place the liver on top. Roll up the saddles and wrap each one in Parma ham. Then wrap each saddle in a doubled sheet of greased foil, twisting the ends tightly to seal. Place the parcels on a baking tray and roast for 15 minutes.

Remove the saddles from the oven and leave to rest for 15 minutes.

Lift the rabbit legs out of the sauce and set aside in a warm place. Strain the sauce through a fine sieve into a clean pan, pressing down on the vegetables and flavourings to extract all the liquid. Whisk in the butter, in small pieces, and add a few drops of tarragon vinegar, the parsley, and pepper to taste.

Unwrap the foil parcels and cut each saddle across into 6 thick slices. Arrange 3 slices on each hot plate with a rabbit leg. Spoon over the sauce and serve.

Suggested garnish: young vegetables

Illustrated on PLATE 13

VOLAILLE À L'INDIENNE
Tandoori-Style Chicken

SERVES 4

4 chicken legs
125 ml/4 fl oz plain yogurt
1 tablespoon tandoori paste
salt
3 slices of white bread
2 cloves of garlic
1 teaspoon chopped fresh mint
1 teaspoon chopped fresh coriander (cilantro)
2 tablespoons olive oil
1 teaspoon curry powder

BRUNO'S NOTES

For this dish, it is important to use the leg of the chicken rather than the breast.

REMOVE the skin from the chicken legs. In a bowl, combine the yogurt, tandoori paste and 4 pinches of salt. Mix well with a spoon. Place the chicken legs in the mixture and leave to marinate in a cool place for 30 minutes.

Meanwhile, put the bread, garlic, mint, coriander, olive oil and curry powder in a food processor and process for 1 minute or until very fine. Put aside on a plate.

Preheat the oven to 180°C/350°F/gas mark 4.

Arrange the chicken legs on a rack in a baking dish and bake for 15 minutes. Remove the chicken and roll it in the bread mixture to coat all over. Put it back on the rack and bake for a further 10 minutes or until nice and golden.

Serve hot.

Suggested garnish: a raw vegetable salad or a simple, crisp 'Iceberg' lettuce salad

CONFIT DE CANARD AU VIN AUX FIGUES

Duck Confit in a Fig Wine Sauce

SERVES 4

4 duck legs
¹/₂ teaspoon Maldon sea salt
freshly ground black pepper
a bunch of fresh thyme
1 bay leaf
1 clove of garlic
750 g/1 lb 10 oz duck fat
150 g/5 oz 'Chutney' de Fruits Secs (page 149)

SAUCE
45 g/1¹/₂ oz shallots or onion
60 g/2 oz button mushrooms
60 g/2 oz celery
60 g/2 oz fennel
20 coriander seeds
15 g/¹/₂ oz/1 tablespoon unsalted butter
100 ml/3¹/₂ fl oz red wine vinegar
1 clove of garlic
200 ml/7 fl oz Jus de Veau (page 18)
100 ml/3¹/₂ fl oz Vin aux Figues (page 152) with 8 figs

BRUNO'S NOTES

The duck fat can be kept in the refrigerator and used again for another confit, if you like.

If you can't get duck fat, you can replace it with 750 g/1 lb 10 oz pork back fat (fresh fatback) melted in a pan with 2 wineglasses of water.

You can use fresh figs as a garnish. Just heat them in the sauce for 10 minutes. Alternatively, serve with Fenouil Braisé (page 116).

THE day before, place the duck legs on a tray and sprinkle over the sea salt, some pepper, the thyme leaves, crumbled bay leaf and chopped garlic. Cover and put in the refrigerator for at least 8 hours.

After a minimum of 8 hours, rinse the duck legs under cold running water. Put them in a large saucepan with the duck fat. Simmer for about 2 hours. Remove from the heat and leave to cool in the fat.

During this time you can prepare the sauce: peel and finely chop the shallots or onion; dice the mushrooms, celery and fennel. Heat the coriander seeds in a small pan until they smell fragrant; set aside.

Melt the butter in a saucepan and cook the prepared vegetables until they are nicely browned, stirring occasionally. Deglaze the pan with the vinegar, stirring well, and boil to reduce until completely evaporated. Stir in the coriander seeds, garlic crushed with the side of a knife, the veal stock, fig wine and 100 ml/3¹/₂ fl oz of water. Bring to the boil and simmer gently for 30 minutes. During this time, add an ice cube every 5 minutes and skim off any scum that rises to the surface.

Strain the sauce through a fine sieve into a small saucepan, pressing down on the vegetables and flavourings to extract all the liquid. Put the figs in the sauce and heat through.

In another small pan, gently heat the dried fruit chutney.

Scrape excess fat from the duck legs and lay them on a baking tray. Place under a preheated moderate grill (broiler) to obtain a golden, crispy crust.

Place a leg of duck confit in the centre of each hot plate with a *quenelle* of chutney and a hot fig on each side. Spoon the sauce round without touching the confit. Serve immediately.

SOURIS D'AGNEAU AUX FLAGEOLETS ET PERSIL PLAT
Braised Lamb Shanks with Parsleyed Flageolets

•

SERVES 4

200 g/7 oz carrots
200 g/7 oz onions
200 g/7 oz celery
3½ tablespoons olive oil
4 lamb shanks
100 ml/3½ fl oz dry white wine
400 g/14 oz canned tomatoes
a bunch of fresh thyme
½ bay leaf
2 cloves of garlic
salt and freshly ground black pepper
45 g/1½ oz turnip
Flageolets au Persil Plat (page 108)

PEEL the carrots and onions; trim the celery. Dice 45 g/1½ oz of each vegetable and set aside. Cut the remainder of the vegetables into chunks for the *braisage*.

Heat the olive oil in a roasting tin or large heavy frying pan and brown the lamb shanks on all sides; transfer them to a large pot. Add the vegetables for the *braisage* to the roasting tin or pan and brown well. Deglaze the tin with the white wine, stirring well, then add the vegetable mixture to the shanks in the large pot, together with the drained tomatoes, the thyme, bay leaf, garlic crushed with the side of a knife, and 200 ml/7 fl oz of water. Simmer for about 2 hours.

Remove the lamb shanks from the pot and keep them hot. Strain the sauce through a fine sieve into a clean pan, pressing down on the vegetables and flavourings to extract all the liquid. Boil until reduced to a nice sauce-like consistency. Season to taste.

Meanwhile, peel and dice the turnip. Cook all the diced vegetables, one by one, in boiling salted water until tender. Drain well and add to the sauce.

Place a lamb shank on the centre of each hot plate, glaze the top with the sauce and spoon the flageolets round. Serve immediately. You can also serve the shanks on a spoonful of Purée d'Hiver (page 118).

PARMENTIER DE CANARD
Duck Confit and Potato Pie

SERVES 4

800 g/1¾ lb potatoes
90 g/3 oz wild mushrooms or open cultivated mushrooms
100 g/3½ oz shallots or onion
2 cloves of garlic
100 ml/3½ fl oz milk
60 g/2 oz/4 tablespoons unsalted butter
freshly ground white pepper
freshly grated nutmeg
vegetable oil
1 tablespoon chopped fresh parsley
1 tablespoon chopped fresh tarragon
4 legs of duck confit
(see recipe for Confit de Canard au Vin aux Figues, page 86)
3 tablespoons Jus de Veau (page 18) or 5 tablespoons soy sauce

BRUNO'S NOTES

In autumn and winter, one-third of the potatoes can be replaced by Jerusalem artichokes.

PEEL the potatoes and cut into large pieces. Put them in a pan of salted water to boil until they feel tender when tested with a thin-bladed knife.

In the meantime, trim and wash the mushrooms well (if using open mushrooms, peel and slice them). Peel and finely chop the shallots or onion and garlic.

Drain the potatoes well and put through a mouli or potato ricer, or mash them until smooth. Heat the milk with the butter, and pepper and nutmeg to taste until boiling, then pour on to the mashed potatoes and mix with a spoon. Set aside.

Preheat the oven to 200°C/400°F/gas mark 6.

Heat a film of oil in a frying pan and cook the mushrooms, shallots and garlic for 5 minutes, stirring occasionally. Add the chopped herbs. Drain in a sieve placed over a bowl to catch the juices.

Spread half of the mashed potatoes in a gratin dish. Peel the crust from the duck confit and take the meat off the bones. Place all the meat on the mashed potatoes in the dish, along with the mushroom mixture. Cover with the rest of the mashed potatoes. Put into the oven to cook for 20 minutes or until nicely golden on top.

Meanwhile, put the juices from the mushrooms in a small saucepan with a veal stock or soy sauce and reduce to a nice sauce-like consistency that will coat the back of a spoon.

Pour the sauce over the gratin and serve.

Suggested garnish: Salade 'Favorite' (page 40) or simply a green salad

ESCALOPE DE FOIE DE VEAU MAURICETTE

Pan-Fried Calf's Liver in My Mother's Style

SERVES 4

800 g/1¾ lb onions
100 g/3½ oz/7 tablespoons unsalted butter
a bunch of fresh thyme
1 tablespoon sliced garlic
a sprig of flat-leaf parsley
salt and freshly ground black pepper
4 slices of calf's liver, weighing 150 g/5 oz each
100 g/3½ oz/⅔ cup flour
vegetable oil
100 ml/3½ fl oz red wine vinegar
1 tablespoon brown sugar
3½ tablespoons Jus de Veau (page 18) or 8 tablespoons soy sauce

PEEL all the onions. Set 200 g/7 oz aside and slice the rest.
Melt all but a small piece of the butter in a saucepan with the thyme, add the sliced onions and cover the pan. Cook over a low to medium heat for about 30 minutes. Remove the lid, turn up the heat and cook the onions until they are a nice brown colour and caramelised. Remove from the heat and set this onion *marmelade* aside.

Blanch the sliced garlic in boiling water for 1 minute; drain and set aside. Blanch the parsley in the same water for 15 seconds; drain and refresh in iced water, then pat dry. Chop the parsley coarsely and set aside. Slice the remaining onions as finely as possible to obtain thin rings; set aside.

Season the slices of liver with salt and pepper, then coat with flour, slapping with your hands to remove excess flour. Heat a film of oil in a frying pan and fry the liver slices for 3 minutes on each side. Remove and keep hot.

Put the blanched garlic into the frying pan with the reserved piece of butter, the red wine vinegar and brown sugar and reduce until syrupy, stirring well. Stir in the veal stock or soy sauce and 125 ml/4 fl oz of water. Bring to the boil and reduce until you obtain a nice sauce-like consistency, but not too thick.

Meanwhile, dip the onion rings in flour on a plate, then deep fry them in hot oil until golden and crisp. Drain on paper towels and keep hot.

Reheat the onion *marmelade*.

Place the liver slices on hot plates and arrange the onion *marmelade* and fried onion rings on top. Stir the parsley into the sauce, spoon the sauce around the liver and serve.

Suggested garnish: Spätzels (page 110) or simply boiled potatoes

PIGEON DES BOIS EN JAMBON DANS SA SAUCE À L'HYDROMEL

Wood Pigeon Wrapped in Parma Ham with a Brandy and Honey Sauce

SERVES 4

100 g/3½ oz pig's caul
malt vinegar
6 oven-ready wood pigeons (squabs)
freshly ground black pepper
6 very thin slices of Parma ham
100 g/3½ oz onions
100 g/3½ oz celeriac (celery root)
60 g/2 oz open mushrooms
vegetable oil
2 cloves of garlic
a bunch of fresh thyme
3½ tablespoons red wine vinegar
100 ml/3½ fl oz Hydromel (page 154)
200 ml/7 fl oz Fond Blanc de Volaille (page 18)
2 tablespoons soy sauce
500 g/1 lb 2 oz white grapes
brandy
30 g/1 oz/2 tablespoons cold unsalted butter

BRUNO'S NOTES

The French love wood pigeon, but it is very difficult to find them in France.

PUT the caul in a bowl of cold water and add about ½ wineglass of malt vinegar. Leave to soak for 30 minutes.

Meanwhile, hold the pigeons over a gas flame to singe any stubble; scrape it off with a small knife. With a small sharp knife, remove the breasts from the birds. Season the breasts with pepper.

Drain the caul, squeeze it dry in your hands and spread it out flat on the work surface. Cut it into 12 pieces (don't worry about any holes).

Wrap each pigeon breast in half a slice of Parma ham and then in a piece of caul. Put aside in the refrigerator.

Chop the pigeon legs and all the carcasses and put them in a large saucepan. Cover with cold water and bring to the boil, then drain and cool under cold running water.

Peel and chop the onions and celeriac; chop the mushrooms. Heat a film of oil in the saucepan and brown the pigeon bones and legs with the onions, celeriac, mushrooms, garlic crushed with the side of a knife and the thyme. Deglaze the pan with the vinegar and the honey wine, stirring well, and reduce until syrupy. Pour over the chicken stock to cover the ingredients and add the soy sauce. Leave to simmer gently for 1 hour.

Meanwhile, with a very small knife, peel the grapes. Remove the seeds as well, if you wish. Put the grapes in a bowl with a little bit of brandy and set aside.

Strain the pigeon stock into a clean pan, pressing down on the bones and flavourings to extract all the liquid. Boil to reduce until you have a nice sauce-like consistency (you should have about 150 ml/5 fl oz of sauce). Set aside.

About 20 minutes before serving, pan-fry the pigeon breasts in a little oil for 4 minutes on each side. Leave them to rest on a dish in a warm place for 5 minutes.

Meanwhile, heat the brandied grapes in a small pan until hot. Reheat the sauce and whisk in the butter, in small pieces.

Put 3 breasts on each hot plate, add the grapes and sauce, and serve.

Suggested garnish: Crêpes de Pommes de Terre et Maïs (page 114)

Illustrated on PLATE 20

CONTRE-FILET DE BOEUF GRILLÉ, CONFIT D'ÉCHALOTTES AUX GRAINES DE MOUTARDE
Grilled Sirloin Steak Topped with a Confit of Shallot and Coarse-Grain Mustard

SERVES 4

500 g/1 lb 2 oz shallots or onions
75 g/2½ oz/5 tablespoons unsalted butter
2 cloves of garlic
a bunch of fresh thyme
2 tablespoons red wine vinegar
2 tablespoons coarse-grain mustard
1 teaspoon chopped fresh flat-leaf parsley
salt and freshly ground black pepper
4 sirloin steaks, each weighing about 150 g/5 oz

BRUNO'S NOTES

This dish does not require any sauce.

If serving with the gnocchi, cook them in boiling salted water for 7 minutes and drain well, then sauté briefly in lightly browned butter (*beurre noisette*) and sprinkle with chopped fresh parsley.

PEEL the shallots or onions and slice them thinly. Melt the butter in a saucepan and add the shallots or onions, garlic crushed with the side of a knife, the thyme and vinegar. Cover the pan and cook on a low heat, stirring from time to time, until the shallots are very soft. This will take about 40 minutes. When cooked, discard the thyme and mix the shallots with the mustard and parsley. Season to taste with salt and pepper. Keep hot.

Heat a cast iron grill pan until very hot, then grill the steaks according to taste.

To serve, top the steaks with the shallot confit.

Suggested garnish: Gnocchis de Pomme de Terre à la Muscade (see recipe for Potage de Potiron, page 29)

CAILLE RÔTIE, PURÉE DE POMMES DE TERRE À L'HUILE DE NOIX

Roasted Quails with Potatoes Mashed in Walnut Oil

SERVES 4

800 g/1¾ lb potatoes, preferably Desirée
salt and freshly ground black pepper
3½ tablespoons vegetable oil
6 oven-ready quails
100 ml/3½ fl oz hot milk
freshly grated nutmeg
2 tablespoons each walnut oil and chopped walnuts
1 tablespoon chopped fresh chives
60 g/2 oz shallots
45 g/1½ oz mushrooms
2 tablespoons tarragon vinegar
a bunch of fresh thyme
1 clove of garlic
2 tablespoons soy sauce

BRUNO'S NOTES

If you think it will take you too long to shape the *quenelles*, just pipe the potatoes on to the middle of the plates and place the pieces of quail on this.

Serve this dish with a simple green salad.

PREHEAT the oven to 220°C/425°F/gas mark 7. Peel the potatoes and cut into large cubes. Put in a saucepan, cover with cold water and add 1 teaspoon of salt. Bring to the boil and cook until soft – about 25 minutes.

Meanwhile, heat a film of vegetable oil in a sauté pan and seal and brown the quails on all sides. Turn the birds on to their backs and season with salt and pepper. Place in the hot oven and roast for 7–10 minutes. When the quails are cooked, remove them from the oven, lift them on to a plate and set aside to rest in a warm place. Reduce the oven temperature to 180°C/350°F/gas mark 4. Drain the potatoes well and spread them out evenly in a roasting tin. Put into the cooler oven to dry for about 10 minutes.

Meanwhile, cut off the quail legs, then cut the breasts from the carcasses. Place all the legs and breasts on a flameproof dish, cover with foil and set aside in a warm place. Chop the quail carcasses.

Pass the potatoes through a mouli or potato ricer into a saucepan. Add the hot milk and 3 pinches of nutmeg and mix very well with a wooden spoon. Mix in the walnut oil, chopped walnuts and chives. Cover and keep warm.

Peel and chop the shallots; chop the mushrooms. Heat a film of vegetable oil in a frying pan and sauté the quail carcasses, shallots and mushrooms for about 5 minutes or until brown. Deglaze with the vinegar, stirring well, then add the thyme, garlic crushed with the side of a knife, the soy sauce and 200 ml/7 fl oz of water. Boil to reduce on a high heat for about 10 minutes or until you have about 8 tablespoons of liquid left. Pass through a fine sieve into a clean pan and bring back to the boil.

Reheat the pieces of quail quickly under the grill (broiler).

To serve, shape 3 *quenelles* of mashed potato on each hot plate, place a quail breast and leg on each *quenelle* and pour over the sauce.

POULE AU POT 'HENRI IV', SAUCE VERTE

Boiled Chicken with Green Sauce

BRUNO'S NOTES

Traditionally, this dish was made with a boiling hen (stewing chicken), which takes much longer to cook.

I really recommend you take the time to make the *miques* with this dish, as they are so good, and can replace the bread.

SERVES 4

400 g/14 oz carrots, preferably baby ones
400 g/14 oz onions
*200 g/7 oz **turnips**, preferably baby ones*
200 g/7 oz celery
400 g/14 oz leeks
1 bay leaf
a bunch of fresh thyme
1 oven-ready chicken, preferably free-range, weighing about 1.4 kg/3 lb
400 g/14 oz unsmoked streaky bacon (slices of mild-cure bacon or salt pork)
Maldon sea salt
a bunch of fresh parsley
4 cloves of garlic
6 black peppercorns
1 clove
Miques (see recipe for Consommé de Cailles et Miques aux Cèpes, page 32), optional
Sauce Verte Girondine (page 20)

PEEL the carrots, onions and turnips and cut into very large chunks (unless they are baby vegetables); cut the celery into chunks. Tie the leeks, bay leaf and thyme together with a piece of string.

Carefully detach the skin from the flesh on the chicken breast, using your hands and starting from the neck opening. Remove the rind from the bacon if necessary, then place a rasher between the skin and the flesh on each breast. Truss the bird with string.

Place the chicken in a large pot, cover with cold water and add a teaspoon of sea salt. Bring to the boil, skimming the surface of all impurities and scum. Add all the vegetables, the herbs, garlic cloves crushed with the side of a knife, the peppercorns and clove. Roll up the remaining bacon rashers and secure with wooden cocktail sticks; add to the pot. Simmer for about 1½ hours.

If you are using the *miques*, put them in to cook with the chicken after it has simmered for 1 hour.

When the chicken is cooked, lift it out of the pot, untruss and cut it into pieces. Place the chicken on hot plates with the vegetables, bacon rolls, *miques* and a little bit of the bouillon. Serve with the sauce verte in a sauceboat, a pot of sea salt, a pepper mill and a pot of mustard.

Suggested garnish: some good country bread – especially delicious spread with duck fat and toasted under the grill (broiler)

Illustrated on PLATE 19

JARRET DE VEAU MIJOTÉ À LA SAUGE ET À L'ORANGE

Osso Bucco

SERVES 4

150 g/5 oz onions
150 g/5 oz carrots
100 g/3½ oz celery
200 g/7 oz tomatoes, preferably plum-type
3½ tablespoons vegetable oil
4 pieces of veal knuckle (veal shank), cut for Osso Bucco, each weighing
350 g/12 oz
30 g/1 oz/2 tablespoons unsalted butter
a strip of orange zest
a bunch of fresh thyme
100 ml/3½ fl oz dry white wine
2 cloves of garlic
4 tablespoons soy sauce
about 1 litre/1¾ pints/1 quart Fond Blanc de Volaille (page 18)
250 ml/8 fl oz olive oil
a large sprig of fresh parsley
1 teaspoon chopped fresh sage
salt and freshly ground black pepper

BRUNO'S NOTES

If you like, blanch some very fine *julienne* of orange zest in boiling water for 5 minutes and drain well, then sprinkle over the dish just before serving. Or sprinkle with chopped fresh chives.

PREHEAT the oven to 180°C/350°F/gas mark 4.
Peel the onions and carrots; trim the celery. Cut two-thirds of the onions and carrots and half of the celery into cubes to make a *mirepoix*. Set the remaining vegetables aside. Cut the tomatoes in half and remove the seeds, then chop the tomatoes.

Heat the vegetable oil in a large sauté pan and sauté the pieces of veal until nicely browned on both sides. Remove them from the pan.

Add the butter to the pan with the vegetable *mirepoix*, the orange zest and thyme and cook until the vegetables are golden. Deglaze the pan with the white wine, stirring well, and reduce for 2 minutes, then add the tomatoes, garlic crushed with the side of a knife and the soy sauce. Stir to mix.

Put back the pieces of veal and pour in enough chicken stock to come 1 cm/½ inch above the level of the ingredients in the pan. Cover and cook in the oven for 1½ hours or until the meat is almost falling off the bones.

Meanwhile, cut the remaining carrots, onions and celery into small cubes for a *brunoise*. Place in a small pan with the olive oil and 100 ml/3½ fl oz of water, put a lid on the pan and cook on a low heat for about 10 minutes or until the vegetables are tender but still firm.

Blanch the parsley in boiling water for 15 seconds; drain and refresh in cold water, then pat dry with paper towels. Tear the parsley leaves into small bits. Set aside.

When the veal is cooked, remove the pieces from the sauce and put aside in a dish. Cover and keep warm. Strain the sauce through a fine sieve into a clean saucepan, pressing down on the vegetables and flavourings to extract all the liquid. Reduce until you have a nice sauce consistency.

Return the pieces of veal to the sauce, together with the drained *brunoise*, the parsley, sage and salt and pepper to taste. Reheat for 5 minutes.

To serve, spoon on to hot plates.

Suggested garnish: Risotto au Safran (page 115)

Illustrated on PLATE 17

POULET DES LANDES RÔTI À L'AIL ET AU CITRON
Corn-Fed Chicken Roasted with Garlic and Lemon

SERVES 4

2 medium-sized heads of garlic
1 lemon
vegetable oil
1 oven-ready corn-fed chicken, weighing about 1.8 kg/4 lb
a few sprigs of fresh thyme or lemon thyme (optional)
salt and freshly ground black pepper
2 heaped tablespoons tomato paste
4 tablespoons soy sauce
1 tablespoon roughly chopped fresh flat-leaf parsley

BRUNO'S NOTES

This is my favourite Sunday lunch. It is a rustic dish, full of flavour. You can peel the garlic cloves before putting them into the chicken, but it is just as nice to squeeze out the flesh from the skins when eating.

The fresh lemon can be replaced by preserved lemon, which is available from Indian shops. This will give a more oriental flavour to the chicken.

My favourite garnishes for this dish are 'Gabaldi' Provençale (page 105) and Gratin Dauphinois (page 106).

DIVIDE the heads of garlic into cloves. Drop the unpeeled cloves into a pan of boiling water and simmer for 15 minutes. Add the whole lemon and simmer for 5 minutes more. Drain. Cut the lemon into quarters.

Preheat the oven to 200°C/400°F/gas mark 6. Put a film of oil in a roasting tin and heat on top of the stove. Add the chicken and seal it all over. Put the lemon quarters, garlic cloves and thyme into the cavity in the chicken with salt and pepper to taste. Turn the chicken so that it rests on one breast.

Place in the oven and roast for 20 minutes, then turn the chicken on to the other breast and roast for another 20 minutes. Finally, turn over on to the back and roast for 15 minutes longer. During roasting, baste frequently with the cooking juices in the tin to keep the chicken moist and crisp the skin. Then take the chicken out of the tin and leave it to rest on a rack in a warm place for 15 minutes.

In the meantime, remove all the fat from the roasting tin and put it over the heat on top of the stove. Add the tomato paste and soy sauce to the cooking juices and stir well. Empty the chicken of the garlic, lemon and thyme and add these to the tin with 4 wineglasses of water. Bring to the boil and boil for 10 minutes, then discard the lemon quarters and thyme stalks. Stir the parsley into the sauce with pepper to taste.

To serve, cut the chicken into pieces, put on a hot dish and pour over the sauce.

TÉTRAS RÔTIES, SALADE TIÈDE DE NAVETS

Roast Grouse on a Warm Turnip Salad

SERVES 4

4 oven-ready grouse
60 g/2 oz shallots
75 g/2½ oz celeriac (celery root)
45 g/1½ oz mushrooms
100 ml/3½ fl oz vegetable oil
500 ml/16 fl oz red wine
3½ tablespoons sherry vinegar or good red wine vinegar
a bunch of fresh thyme
½ bay leaf, 2 cloves of garlic, 6 green peppercorns
200 ml/7 fl oz Jus de Veau (page 18)
salt and freshly ground black pepper
400 g/14 oz turnips
2 tablespoons walnut oil
1 teaspoon chopped fresh chives

BRUNO'S NOTES

Every year, the opening of the shooting season for grouse in the UK is quite an event. For this dish, choose fresh grouse that were shot 2–3 days previously, when the flavour will be strong enough.

Do not put the dirty backbones into the sauce as they will give some bitterness. The addition of the ice cubes helps with the elimination of the impurities from the sauce.

Purée d'Hiver (page 118) is a good garnish for this dish.

PREHEAT the oven to 200°C/400°F/gas mark 6.
   Cut off the feet of the grouse at the joints, and trim any stubble left using a small knife. Set the birds aside.

Peel and chop the shallots and celeriac. Chop the mushrooms. In a saucepan, heat half of the vegetable oil and cook the chopped vegetables until nice and brown, then pour in the wine and vinegar and add the thyme, bay leaf, garlic crushed with the side of a knife and the peppercorns. Bring to the boil and reduce until you have only 2 tablespoons of liquid left. Stir in the veal stock, and leave to simmer very gently while you roast the grouse.

Season the grouse inside and out. Heat the remaining vegetable oil in a sauté pan and seal and brown the grouse on each side for 30 seconds, then turn the birds on to their backs. Roast in the oven for about 10 minutes. When cooked, leave the grouse to rest in a warm place for about 5 minutes.

Meanwhile, peel the turnips and slice them thinly with a large sharp knife, or a mandoline. Blanch the turnip slices in boiling salted water for 3–4 minutes; drain and refresh in iced water. Set aside on paper towels.

Carve the legs and breasts from the grouse, season the pieces and put on a plate. Cover with foil and set aside in a warm place. Chop the grouse carcasses (excluding the backbones), add to the sauce with 2 cracked ice cubes and simmer for 5 minutes.

Strain the sauce through a fine sieve into a clean pan and reduce over a brisk heat, skimming from time to time, until nice and shiny.

Heat the walnut oil in a pan, add the turnips and mix gently with a fork. When the turnips are hot, add the chopped chives.

To serve, spoon the turnips on to the centre of hot plates, place the grouse breasts and legs on top and pour the sauce around.

Râble et Cuisse de Lapin aux Tomates Douces

Roasted Saddle and Leg of Rabbit with Sun-Dried Tomatoes and Parma Ham
(recipe page 84)

PLATE 13

Filet de Chevreuil dans une Sauce Réglisse et Vin Rouge

Roast Fillet of Venison in a Liquorice-Flavoured Red Wine Sauce
(recipe page 80)

PLATE 14

Queue de Boeuf Mijotée aux Pruneaux et au Vinaigre

Braised Oxtail with Prunes and Vinegar
(recipe page 82)

PLATE 15

Longe de Porc en Cocotte à la Vanille

Loin of Pork 'Pot-Roasted' with Vanilla
(recipe page 81)

PLATE 16

Jarret de Veau Mijoté à la Sauge et à l'Orange

Osso Bucco
(recipe page 94)

PLATE 17

Faisan Rôti à la Choucroûte Fraîche, Son Jus à l'Abricot

Roast Pheasant with Braised Cabbage and an Apricot Sauce
(recipe page 98)

PLATE 18

Poule au Pot 'Henri IV', Sauce Verte

Boiled Chicken with Green Sauce
(recipe page 93)

PLATE 19

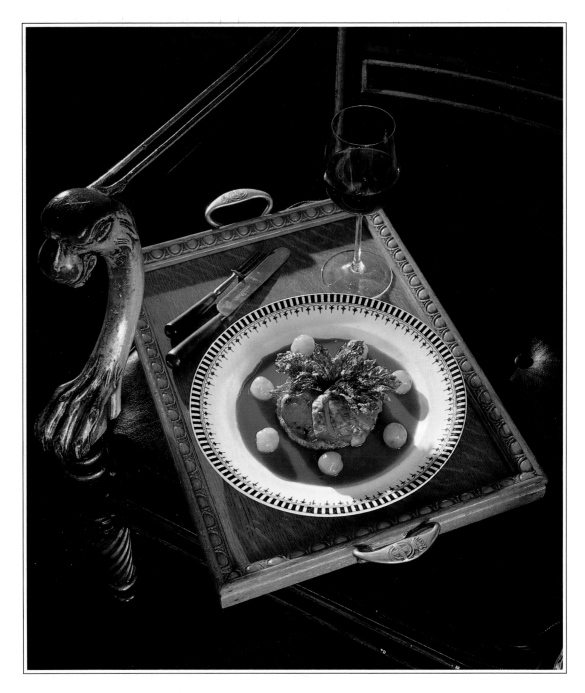

Pigeon des Bois en Jambon dans Sa Sauce à l'Hydromel

Wood Pigeon Wrapped in Parma Ham with a Brandy and Honey Sauce
(recipe page 90)

PLATE 20

PINTADE RÔTIE AU CÉLERI ET SES TARTINES
Roast Guinea Fowl with Celery and Soft Cheese Toasts

BRUNO'S NOTES

When I make this dish at home, I can't wait to eat a *tartine*, before the rest, because it's so irresistible!

SERVES 4

2 oven-ready guinea fowl, weighing about 1 kg/2¼ lb each, with their livers
salt and freshly ground black pepper
4 cloves of garlic
60 g/2 oz chicken livers
2 Petit Suisses cheeses (unsweetened)
a bunch of fresh parsley
a bunch of fresh thyme
vegetable oil
1 bunch of celery
a wineglass of dry white wine
3 tablespoons Jus de Veau (page 18) or 5 tablespoons soy sauce
45 g/1½ oz/3 tablespoons cold unsalted butter (optional)
4 slices of brown bread

PREHEAT the oven to 200°C/400°F/gas mark 6. Wipe the guinea fowls inside and out. Season the insides with salt and pepper. Chop 2 of the garlic cloves, and cut the chicken livers into 2 or 3 pieces. Stuff each guinea fowl with a soft cheese, a guinea fowl liver, half the chicken livers and chopped garlic, and half the parsley and thyme. Truss the birds with string.

Put a film of oil in a roasting tin and heat on top of the stove. Seal the guinea fowls all over. Turn the birds on to one breast and put into the oven to roast for 10 minutes. Turn the birds on to the other breast and roast for 10 minutes longer, then turn on to the back for a final 10 minutes of roasting. During the roasting time, baste the birds frequently with the cooking juices to keep them moist and to give them a crisp brown skin.

While the guinea fowl are roasting, cut the celery into 1 cm/½ inch pieces. Peel and finely chop the remaining garlic.

Remove the birds from the oven and set aside to rest in a warm place. Pour off all the fat from the roasting tin, leaving the cooking juices. Add the pieces of celery to the tin and cook over a low heat on top of the stove until golden brown. Deglaze the tin with the wine, stirring well, and bring to the boil. Add 600 ml/1 pint/2½ cups of water, the veal stock or soy sauce and the chopped garlic. Boil for 10 minutes. If liked, finish the sauce by whisking in the butter, in small pieces (this will give the sauce a nice shine). Keep hot.

Toast the bread. Empty the stuffing from the guinea fowl into a bowl (discard the herbs) and mash with a fork. Spread on to the toast and cut each slice into triangles.

Cut the guinea fowl into pieces and put a breast and a leg on each hot plate. Pour the celery sauce over and put 2 triangles of toast on each side of each plate. Serve immediately.

Suggested garnish: Canellonis d'Épinards et Artichauts (page 117)

FAISAN RÔTI À LA CHOUCROÛTE FRAÎCHE, SON JUS À L'ABRICOT

Roast Pheasant with Braised Cabbage and an Apricot Sauce

SERVES 4

450 g/1 lb white cabbage
1 tablespoon coarse sea salt
10 juniper berries
vegetable oil
2 oven-ready pheasants, preferably hens, barded with pork fat
celery salt
freshly ground black pepper
400 ml/14 fl oz white wine from Alsace
100 ml/3½ fl oz white wine vinegar
3 cloves of garlic
½ bay leaf
90 g/3 oz dried apricots
60 g/2 oz/4 tablespoons cold unsalted butter
1 onion
75 g/2½ oz shallots
100 g/3½ oz celery
a branch of fresh thyme
60 g/2 oz tomatoes, preferably plum-type
1 tablespoon soy sauce

TRIM and core the cabbage, and chop it finely. Place it in a bowl and season with the sea salt. Heat the juniper berries in a small pan for a few seconds, just until they are aromatic, then add them to the cabbage. Mix very well with your hands, to distribute the salt and juniper berries evenly in the cabbage, and leave at room temperature for 1 hour.

Preheat the oven to 200°C/400°F/gas mark 6.

Heat a film of vegetable oil in a roasting tin on top of the stove and seal the pheasants on all sides. Finally, turn the birds on to their backs and season with celery salt and pepper. Put into the oven to roast for about 20 minutes. During this time, spoon the fat and cooking juices over the birds occasionally to give them a nice golden colour and shine.

While the pheasants are roasting, turn the cabbage into a colander and rinse under cold running water, then place it in a saucepan with 300 ml/10 fl oz of the white wine, the vinegar, 2 cloves of garlic crushed with the side of a knife, and the bay leaf. Cover the pan and leave to cook over a moderate heat, stirring occasionally, for 30 minutes. At the end of this time, the cabbage should be just tender but still crisp to the bite.

Meanwhile, cut the apricots into small dice and soak in warm water for 10 minutes. Drain and pat dry on paper towels. Set aside.

When the pheasants have finished roasting, leave them to rest in a warm place for 10 minutes. Then carve the breasts and legs and keep hot. I suggest that the drumsticks not be served as they are tough; instead, use them for the sauce. Chop the drumsticks and the pheasant carcasses.

In a large saucepan, melt 15 g/½ oz/1 tablespoon of the butter with 1 tablespoon of vegetable oil. Add the chopped onion, shallots and celery and cook until they are nicely coloured, then add the pheasant drumsticks and carcasses, the remaining garlic crushed with the side of a knife, and the thyme. Cook, stirring, for 5 minutes. Deglaze with the remaining white wine, stirring well, then reduce by half.

Remove the seeds from the tomatoes and chop them coarsely; add to the saucepan with the soy sauce and 400 ml/14 fl oz of water. Bring back to the boil and reduce by half again.

Increase the oven temperature to 230°C/450°F/gas mark 8.

Strain the sauce through a fine sieve into a small saucepan, pressing down on the bones and flavourings to extract all the liquid. Skim off all the impurities that rise to the surface, then season with pepper and whisk in the remaining butter, in small pieces. Add the dried apricots to the sauce. Keep hot.

Reheat the pheasant breasts and thighs in the hot oven for 2–3 minutes.

To serve, place a bed of cabbage in the middle of each hot plate and top with a pheasant thigh and a breast cut into 3 pieces. Pour the sauce around.
Suggested garnish: Gratin Dauphinois (page 106)

Illustrated on PLATE 18

Petites moussakas

Nage de légumes aux fines herbes

Petits choux farcis grand-mère

'Gabaldi' provençale

Gratin dauphinois

Pommes de terre frites

Purée de pommes de terre

Pommes de terre à l'anis

Flageolets au persil plat

Gratin de macaronis aux truffes

Macaronis farcis

Spaghettis de légumes

Spätzels

Ratatouille

Ragoût de fèves à la sariette

Polenta grillée

Endives braisées à l'orange et au poivre

Etuvée de carottes au cumin

Crêpes de pommes de terre et maïs

Risotto au safran

Oignons au four au gingembre

Fenouil braisé

Canellonis d'épinards et artichauts

Purée d'hiver

Petits pois à la française

Palets à l'ail

CHAPTER FIVE

Garnitures

GARNISHES

I have a philosophy about vegetable dishes – I prefer a simple and unique garnish for a main dish, rather than the same side selection of vegetables whatever the dish is. For the fish and meat dishes in the book, I have suggested what I think is the appropriate garnish. In this chapter, I give a good range of garnishes from which you can choose, according to your taste, your time limitations and the availability of the ingredients. This will help develop your own sense of combining flavours, textures and colours. After all, there is more to cooking than the sum of the recipe. Some of the garnishes here can also be served as light vegetarian dishes.

PETITES MOUSSAKAS
Individual Moussakas

SERVES 4

60 g/2 oz onions
3½ tablespoons olive oil
100 g/3½ oz minced lamb (ground lamb)
1 teaspoon tomato paste
2 tablespoons soy sauce
mild curry powder
½ teaspoon chopped fresh mint
½ teaspoon chopped fresh coriander (cilantro)
300 g/10 oz potatoes
100 ml/3½ fl oz milk
freshly grated nutmeg
4 slices of aubergine (eggplant), each 1 cm/½ inch thick
4 cloves of garlic
3½ tablespoons double cream (heavy cream)
150 g/5 oz courgettes (zucchini)

PREHEAT the oven to 180°C/350°F/gas mark 4.
Peel and finely chop the onions. Heat a film of olive oil in a saucepan, add the onions and cook until they are golden brown. Add the lamb, tomato paste, soy sauce and a pinch of curry powder and cook for about 30 minutes, stirring frequently to break up the meat. Stir in the mint and coriander.

While the lamb mixture is cooking, prepare the potatoes. Peel them and cut into chunks, then cook in boiling salted water until soft – about 25 minutes depending on the quality of the potatoes. Drain well in a colander, then spread out in a roasting tin. Put into the oven to dry for 10 minutes.

Put the milk into a saucepan and bring to the boil. Remove from the heat. Pass the potatoes through a mouli or potato ricer into the milk and mix well with a wooden spoon. Add nutmeg to taste. Set aside.

Heat a film of olive oil in a non-stick frying pan and fry the aubergine slices until golden brown on both sides. Deglaze the pan with ½ wineglass of water, stirring well, then cook for a further 5 minutes. Set aside.

Blanch the garlic in boiling water for 3 minutes. Drain and return to the pan. Add the cream and cook until the garlic is very soft, then liquidise to obtain a thick garlic cream.

Cut the courgettes lengthways into 2 mm/scant ⅛ inch thick slices. Blanch them in boiling salted water for 1 minute; drain and refresh in iced water, then pat dry with paper towels.

Take 4 metal cylinders, each 5 cm/2 inches in diameter and 5 cm/2 inches high, and place each on a small square of foil. Wrap the foil up around the base of the cylinder and place these moulds on a baking tray. Place an aubergine slice in the bottom of each mould, then line the side of each mould with a courgette slice, placing it horizontally. Put half the mashed potato into the moulds, packing it down evenly, then add the lamb mixture and finally the rest of the mashed potato, making a little hollow in the centre. Spread the garlic cream on the top.

Bake the moussakas for 5 minutes.

To serve, place a moussaka on a hot plate. Unwrap the foil at the base of the mould and, holding one side of the foil, slide the moussaka off it, then carefully lift off the metal cylinder.

NAGE DE LÉGUMES AUX FINES HERBES
Poached Vegetables with Herbs

SERVES 4

150 g/5 oz cucumber
salt and freshly ground black pepper
100 g/3½ oz tomatoes, preferably plum-type
100 g/3½ oz carrots
100 g/3½ oz onions
150 g/5 oz celery
100 g/3½ oz leeks
150 g/5 oz bulb of fennel
300 ml/10 fl oz Nage de Légumes (page 19)
1 clove of garlic
3 tablespoons double cream (heavy cream)
60 g/2 oz/4 tablespoons cold unsalted butter
½ teaspoon chopped fresh parsley
½ teaspoon chopped fresh chives
½ teaspoon chopped fresh dill

BRUNO'S NOTES

This is a good accompaniment for plainly cooked fish dishes.

If you prefer, you can season with ground cumin or mild curry powder instead of black pepper.

CUT the cucumber in half lengthways and scoop out the seeds with a teaspoon. Cut the halves across into 5 mm/¼ inch thick slices. Spread the slices on a tray, sprinkle over 4 pinches of salt and set aside.

Skin, seed and dice the tomatoes. Peel or trim the remaining vegetables and cut them into 5 mm/¼ inch thick slices.

Rinse the cucumber slices under cold running water and dry them on paper towels.

Bring the nage to the boil in a saucepan. Add the carrots, onions, celery, leeks, fennel and garlic slightly crushed with the side of a knife. Simmer for about 8 minutes. Remove the pan from the heat. Discard the garlic, then stir in the cream. Whisk in the butter in small pieces.

Add the cucumber, tomatoes, herbs, and salt and pepper to taste and mix well. Serve immediately.

PETITS CHOUX FARCIS GRAND-MÈRE
Old-Style Stuffed Cabbage

SERVES 4

2 slices of white bread
3½ tablespoons milk
100 g/3½ oz onions
45 g/1½ oz/3 tablespoons unsalted butter or duck fat
45 g/1½ oz chicken livers
1 clove of garlic
100 g/3½ oz Parma ham or unsmoked streaky bacon (mild-cure bacon
or salt pork)
1 egg
salt and freshly ground black pepper
1 tablespoon chopped fresh parsley
1 Savoy cabbage
Fond Blanc de Volaille (page 18) or water

SOAK the bread in the milk in a bowl; squeeze dry. Peel and chop the onions. Melt the butter or duck fat in a frying pan and sweat the onions until softened without colouring. Add the chicken livers and garlic crushed with the side of a knife and cook for 2 minutes, stirring. Turn the mixture into a food processor and add the bread, Parma ham or bacon and egg. Process for 5 seconds. Season with pepper and add the parsley. Set this *farce* aside.

Separate 8 large, outside leaves from the cabbage. Chop the rest of the cabbage, discarding the core. Blanch the cabbage leaves in boiling salted water for 3 minutes, then drain and cool in iced water. Repeat the same operation with the chopped cabbage. Dry the leaves on paper towels, and squeeze dry the chopped cabbage. Mix the chopped cabbage with the *farce*.

Cut out 4 pieces of muslin or cheesecloth, each about 20 cm/8 inches square. Lay one square of muslin or cheesecloth on the work surface and arrange 2 cabbage leaves on top, overlapping them. Spoon one-quarter of the *farce* into the centre of the cabbage and wrap the leaves around to form a ball. Enclose the ball in the cloth and tie tightly with string. Repeat to make 3 more balls.

Cook the cabbage parcels in simmering chicken stock for 15 minutes, or steam over boiling water.

Unwrap and serve hot.

BRUNO'S NOTES

If you like, remove 4 extra cabbage leaves and blanch them, then wrap them around the cabbage balls just before serving, for a better presentation.

Illustrated opposite

Petits Choux Farcis Grand-Mère

Old-Style Stuffed Cabbage

PLATE 21

Spaghettis de Légumes

Vegetable Spaghetti
(recipe page 110)

PLATE 22

Endives Braisées à l'Orange et au Poivre

———————

Braised Chicory Flavoured with Orange and Green Peppercorns
(recipe page 113)

PLATE 23

'Gabaldi' Provençale

Gratin of Provençal Vegetables

PLATE 24

'GABALDI' PROVENÇALE
Gratin of Provençale Vegetables

SERVES 4

300 g/10 oz large courgettes (zucchini)
400 g/14 oz aubergines (eggplant)
salt and freshly ground black pepper
300 g/10 oz ripe tomatoes, preferably plum-type
3½ tablespoons olive oil
a bunch of fresh thyme
2 cloves of garlic
1 tablespoon chopped fresh basil

PREHEAT the oven to 220°C/425°F/gas mark 7.
Cut the courgettes into 5 mm/¼ inch thick slices. Blanch them in boiling salted water for 2 minutes, then drain and refresh in iced water. Pat dry with paper towels.

Cut the aubergines into 5 mm/¼ inch thick slices. Put them in a colander, sprinkle liberally with salt and leave to drain for 10 minutes. Rinse the slices under cold running water and pat dry with paper towels.

Slice the tomatoes thinly.

Arrange the courgette, aubergine and tomato slices, alternately and overlapping each other, in a gratin dish. Pour over the olive oil and crumble over the thyme. Finely chop the garlic and sprinkle on top of the sliced vegetables. Season with salt and pepper.

Place in the hot oven and bake for 10 minutes.

Sprinkle over the basil and serve.

Illustrated opposite

105

GRATIN DAUPHINOIS
Sliced Potatoes Baked in Cream

SERVES 4

200 ml/7 fl oz milk
200 ml/7 fl oz double cream (heavy cream)
salt and freshly ground black pepper
freshly grated nutmeg
1 kg/2¼ lb potatoes
60 g/2 oz/4 tablespoons unsalted butter, softened
3 cloves of garlic

PREHEAT the oven to 180°C/350°F/gas mark 4.
Boil the milk, and mix it with the cream in a large bowl. Season with salt and pepper and add 2 pinches of nutmeg. Peel the potatoes and cut them into 5 mm/¼ inch thick slices. Mix with the milk and cream.

Spread the soft butter all over the inside of a gratin dish, then scatter over the very finely chopped garlic. Layer the sliced potatoes in the dish, overlapping them, then pour over the cream and milk mixture.

Place in the oven and bake for about 45 minutes or until the potatoes are tender (test with the tip of a sharp knife) and the top is golden. Serve hot.

BRUNO'S NOTES

This is very good with a simple roast, especially leg or shoulder of lamb.

POMMES DE TERRE FRITES
French Fries

SERVES 4

1.2 kg/3 lb potatoes
1 litre/1¾ pints/1 quart groundnut oil (peanut oil)
salt

PEEL the potatoes. Square them with a knife on a chopping board, then cut into 1 cm/½ inch thick slices. Cut each slice into 1 cm/½ inch sticks. Place the potatoes in a basin of cold water and rinse them very well, then drain and pat dry on a kitchen cloth.

Heat the oil to a temperature of 130°C/265°F. Put the potatoes into a frying basket and blanch them in the oil until they become slightly soft (test by removing one, cooling it and then squeezing it between two fingers: it should still have some resistance). Drain the potatoes.

Reheat the oil to 180°C/350°F, which is very hot. Lower the basket of potatoes back into the oil and fry until golden and crisp. Drain them very well in the basket or on paper towels. Tip the potatoes on to a paper napkin in a dish, season with salt and serve.

PURÉE DE POMMES DE TERRE
Mashed Potatoes

SERVES 4

800 g/1¾ lb potatoes
salt
150 g/5 oz/10 tablespoons cold unsalted butter
150 ml/5 fl oz hot milk
freshly grated nutmeg

BRUNO'S NOTES

Potatoes for mashing should have a floury texture, and I think that the best British varieties are Desirée, Pentland Crown and Pentland Hawk.

PREHEAT the oven to 180°C/350°F/gas mark 4.
Peel the potatoes and cut into chunks. Put them in a saucepan and cover with cold water. Add a little salt. Bring to the boil and simmer gently until the potatoes are soft – about 25 minutes depending on the quality of the potatoes. Test them with the tip of a sharp knife.

Drain the potatoes in a colander and spread them out in a roasting tin. Put them into the oven to dry for 10 minutes.

Pass the potatoes through a mouli or potato ricer into a clean saucepan. Add the butter in small pieces, stirring with a wooden spoon. Slowly pour in the hot milk, stirring well, then season with 2 pinches of nutmeg. Serve hot.

POMMES DE TERRE À L'ANIS
Anise-Flavoured Boiled Potatoes

SERVES 4

100 g/3½ oz onions
3½ tablespoons olive oil
1 clove of garlic
a bunch of fresh thyme
3 star anise
600 g/1¼ lb small new potatoes, ideally all the same size (peeled weight)
salt and freshly ground black pepper

BRUNO'S NOTES

If new potatoes are not available, you can use larger main-crop, all-purpose varieties. Cut each potato into quarters, then 'turn' each piece into a barrel shape (see page 13 for instructions).

PEEL and chop the onions. Heat the olive oil in a sauté pan and add the onions, chopped garlic, thyme and star anise. Sweat over a low heat until the onions are softened but not browned.

Add the potatoes and enough water to cover them. Season with salt and pepper. Cover the pan and simmer for about 20 minutes or until the potatoes are tender.

Drain the potatoes and serve hot.

FLAGEOLETS AU PERSIL PLAT
Flageolets with Parsley

SERVES 4

250 g/9 oz/1¼ cups dried flageolets
100 g/3½ oz onions
100 g/3½ oz carrots
100 g/3½ oz celery
75 g/2½ oz/5 tablespoons unsalted butter
1 clove of garlic
a bunch of fresh thyme
1 litre/1¾ pints/1 quart Fond Blanc de Volaille (page 18) or water
salt and freshly ground black pepper
1 tablespoon chopped fresh flat-leaf parsley

SOAK the flageolets overnight in a large bowl of cold water.
Drain the flageolets. Peel the onions and carrots and cut into 5 mm/
¼ inch dice. Dice the celery too.

In a large saucepan, heat half of the butter and cook the diced vegetables
with 2 tablespoons of water over a very low heat for about 25 minutes, until
very soft but not coloured. Add the garlic crushed with the side of a knife,
the thyme and the flageolets and stir to mix. Pour in the chicken stock and
leave to cook for about 1½ hours or until the flageolets are soft to the bite
and the juices are quite thick.

Season with salt and pepper, and stir in the parsley and the remaining
butter. Serve hot.

BRUNO'S NOTES

The cooking time for the
flageolets can vary according
to how dry the beans are, so
test them from time to time
to avoid overcooking.

GRATIN DE MACARONIS
AUX TRUFFES
Macaroni and Truffle Gratin

SERVES 4

40 g/1⅓ oz/2½ tablespoons unsalted butter
20 g/⅔ oz/2½ tablespoons flour
200 ml/7 fl oz milk
200 ml/7 fl oz double cream (heavy cream)
white pepper
200 g/7 oz short macaroni
45 g/1½ oz canned or bottled truffle peelings
60-90 g/2-3 oz Gruyère cheese

BRUNO'S NOTES

If you prefer, you can finish
the dish under the grill
(broiler) rather than in the
oven, as long as the sauce and
macaroni are hot.

This dish is a classic from
the Lyons area of France.

MELT the butter in a saucepan and mix in the flour with a whisk. Cook for 2 minutes, then leave this *roux* to cool.

In another saucepan, bring the milk and cream to the boil. Pour over the *roux*, stirring well with the whisk. Return to the heat and leave to simmer for 20 minutes, stirring from time to time. Season to taste with pepper.

Preheat the oven to 220°C/425°F/gas mark 7.

While the sauce is simmering, bring a large pan of salted water to the boil and cook the macaroni until *al dente*. Drain in a colander and rinse under hot water.

Mix the macaroni with the sauce, then stir in the truffle peelings. Turn the mixture into a gratin dish and sprinkle over the grated Gruyère.

Place in the hot oven (see Notes) and cook until the top is nicely browned. Serve hot.

MACARONIS FARCIS
Pasta Stuffed with Chicken and Herbs

SERVES 4

180 g/6 oz large pasta shapes for stuffing (rigatoni,
jumbo shells and so on)
vegetable oil
100 g/3½ oz onions
100 g/3½ oz mushrooms
45 g/1½ oz/3 tablespoons unsalted butter
1 clove of garlic
1 tablespoon chopped fresh parsley
1 teaspoon chopped fresh sage
100 g/3½ oz skinned, boned chicken breast
salt and freshly ground black pepper

COOK the pasta shapes in a large pan of boiling water until *al dente*. Drain in a colander and refresh under cold running water until completely cold. Then place the pasta in a large bowl, sprinkle over a few drops of oil and mix to coat them. Set aside.

Peel and finely chop the onions; finely chop the mushrooms. Melt the butter in a large sauté pan and sweat the onions and mushrooms for about 8 minutes without letting them brown. Stir in the finely chopped garlic and the herbs and cook for a further 2 minutes. Turn the mixture into a bowl and put aside.

Cut the chicken into very small pieces, then with a heavy knife chop the chicken meat finely. Mix the chicken meat with the mushroom and onion mixture, and season with salt and pepper.

Put the chicken mixture into a piping bag fitted with a plain tube, and pipe into the pasta shapes to fill them.

Cook the stuffed pasta in a steamer for 5 minutes, and serve hot.

BRUNO'S NOTES

These stuffed pasta shapes are a delicious accompaniment for a roast. Turn them in the juices in the roasting tin before serving. Or serve them as a main dish with a tarragon cream sauce (see the recipe for Fond Blanc de Volaille, page 18).

SPAGHETTIS DE LÉGUMES
Vegetable Spaghetti

SERVES 4

200 g/7 oz carrots
200 g/7 oz courgettes (zucchini)
200 g/7 oz mooli or daikon (white radish)
200 g/7 oz leeks
30 g/1 oz/2 tablespoons unsalted butter
1 tablespoon chopped fresh chervil
1 teaspoon chopped fresh chives
salt and freshly ground black pepper

PEEL the carrots and trim the ends so they are all about 12 cm/5 inches long. With a sharp knife, trim the sides to obtain square shapes. Cut each carrot lengthways into thin slices and then into thin strips to resemble spaghetti.

Repeat the same operation with the courgettes and mooli.

Trim off the ends of the leeks so they are all 12 cm/5 inches long. Cut them in half lengthways, then holding down the leaves, cut into fine, long strips.

Blanch the vegetables one at a time in boiling salted water: carrots for 3 minutes, mooli 2 minutes, courgettes 2 minutes and leeks 3 minutes. Drain and refresh in iced water, then pat dry with paper towels.

In a sauté pan, melt the butter and add all the vegetables and the herbs. Mix with a fork, season with salt and pepper, and serve.

Illustrated on PLATE 22

SPÄTZELS
Tiny Egg Dumplings

SERVES 4

75 g/2½ oz/5 tablespoons unsalted butter
250 g/9 oz/1⅔ cups flour
2 eggs
1 egg yolk
½ teaspoon salt
freshly grated nutmeg
125 ml/4 fl oz milk

PUT 30 g/1 oz/2 tablespoons of the butter into a small pan and heat until it has melted and turned a light brown (*noisette*). Pour it quickly into a

BRUNO'S NOTES

Normally, spätzels are made on a wooden board with a palette knife (narrow metal spatula), but that operation is quite skilled so here I have given a simpler method as a good alternative.

large bowl and leave to cool slightly, then add the flour, whole eggs, egg yolk, salt and 2 pinches of nutmeg. Starting in the centre, mix the ingredients together with a wooden spoon, slowly pouring the milk into the centre. Beat the mixture very well with the spoon for 5 minutes. The consistency should be like a thick sauce or thick pancake batter.

Bring a large pan of salted water to the boil.

Put the mixture into a colander, hold it over the pan and press the mixture through the holes in the colander with a spatula into the water, to make little worm-like dumplings. When the spätzels rise to the surface, they are cooked. Lift out the spätzels with a slotted spoon and refresh under cold running water. Tip them on to paper towels to drain.

Melt the remaining butter in a frying pan, add the spätzels and sauté quickly until golden brown. Serve immediately.

RATATOUILLE

SERVES 4

150 g/5 oz onions
120 g/4 oz red sweet pepper
120 g/4 oz yellow sweet pepper
200 g/7 oz courgettes (zucchini)
300 g/10 oz aubergines (eggplant)
200 g/7 oz tomatoes, preferably plum-type
100 ml/3½ fl oz olive oil
2 cloves of garlic
a bunch of fresh thyme
salt and freshly ground black pepper

PEEL the onions and cut them into 1 cm/½ inch cubes.

With a vegetable peeler, thinly peel the sweet peppers. Cut them in half and discard the core and seeds, then cut the flesh into 1 cm/½ inch cubes.

Cut the courgettes and aubergines into 1 cm/½ inch cubes. Skin, seed and dice the tomatoes.

Prepare a tray topped with paper towels.

Heat a film of olive oil in a frying pan and cook the onions and sweet peppers together for about 8 minutes, then remove from the pan with a slotted spoon and drain on the paper towels.

In the same pan, heat another film of olive oil and cook the aubergines with 4 tablespoons of water for about 2 minutes. Add the courgettes and cook for a further 5 minutes.

Return the onions and peppers to the pan together with the tomatoes, chopped garlic and thyme. Stir well and cook for 5 minutes longer.

Season with salt and pepper, and serve.

BRUNO'S NOTES

I like ratatouille made this way, so that all the vegetables keep their texture, rather than turning into a stew.

RAGOÛT DE FÈVES À LA SARIETTE
Broad Beans in a Savory Sauce

SERVES 4

2.4 kg/5¼ lb broad beans (fava beans)
1 tablespoon chopped fresh flat-leaf parsley
100 g/3½ oz onions
60 g/2 oz/4 tablespoons unsalted butter
1 clove of garlic
a bunch of fresh savory or thyme
3½ tablespoons dry white wine
150 ml/5 fl oz Nage de Légumes (page 19) or water
1 tablespoon double cream (heavy cream)
salt and freshly ground black pepper

SHELL the broad beans (there should be about 600 g/1¼ lb). Blanch them in boiling salted water for 30 seconds, then lift them out with a slotted spoon and plunge them immediately into iced water. Drain, then peel the skins off the beans. Set aside.

Put the parsley into a small metal sieve and dip into the bean blanching water. Blanch for 5 seconds, then remove and leave to drain.

Peel and chop the onions. Heat half of the butter in a saucepan and add the onions, finely chopped garlic and the savory. Cook over a low heat until the onions are softened, without browning. Deglaze the pan with the white wine, stirring well, then bring to the boil and boil for 2 minutes.

Pour in the nage and bring back to the boil. Add the broad beans, parsley and cream and heat for 3–5 minutes, stirring occasionally.

Remove from the heat and stir in the remaining butter in small pieces. Season with salt and pepper, and serve.

BRUNO'S NOTES

It is a shame that nowadays broad beans are not used more often as they are particularly delicious.

POLENTA GRILLÉE
Grilled Polenta

SERVES 4

100 g/3½ oz unsmoked streaky bacon (slices of
mild-cure bacon or salt pork)
1 teaspoon salt
150 g/5 oz/1 cup + 3 tablespoons polenta or yellow cornmeal
1 teaspoon chopped fresh sage
1 teaspoon chopped fresh parsley
20 g/⅔ oz/1½ tablespoons unsalted butter
olive oil

BRUNO'S NOTES

I love this turned into a main dish, with tomato sauce and goat's cheese on top.

REMOVE the rind from the bacon, if necessary, then cut the rashers across into very fine *lardons*. Place them in a small pan, cover with water and boil for 1 minute. Drain the bacon, rinse under cold running water and dry on paper towels.

Bring 600 ml/1 pint/2½ cups of water to the boil in a saucepan. Add the salt, then add the polenta in a stream, stirring constantly. Cook for 20 minutes, stirring from time to time.

Add the bacon, herbs and butter to the polenta and mix well. Spread the mixture in a shallow square tin to make a layer about 1.5 cm/⅝ inch thick. Leave until cold and set.

Cut the polenta into shapes – rounds, rectangles or squares, as you like. Brush the shapes with olive oil and grill (broil) on both sides until golden brown. Serve hot.

ENDIVES BRAISÉES À L'ORANGE ET AU POIVRE

Braised Chicory Flavoured with Orange and Green Peppercorns

SERVES 4

4 heads of chicory (Belgian endive)
60 g/2 oz/4 tablespoons unsalted butter
1 teaspoon brown sugar
finely grated zest and juice of ½ *orange*
4 tablespoons tarragon or white wine vinegar
1 clove of garlic
½ *teaspoon green peppercorns*
salt

BRUNO'S NOTES

This dish is excellent with any red meat, but particularly with game. If the sauce is too sweet to your taste after reducing, add 1 teaspoon of tarragon vinegar and boil for 10 seconds.

PREHEAT the oven to 190°C/375°F/gas mark 5.
Cut each head of chicory in half lengthways and cut out the hard core in the middle.

Put the butter in a roasting tin and melt on top of the stove. Add the chicory halves and cook quickly until golden on both sides.

Add the brown sugar, orange zest and juice, the vinegar, garlic crushed with the side of a knife, and a wineglass of water. Lightly crush the green peppercorns in your hand and add to the pan with salt to taste. Stir gently to mix the flavourings with the chicory.

Bring to the boil, then cover the tin with foil and put into the oven to cook for 20 minutes or until the chicory is just tender.

Lift the chicory out of the tin with a slotted spoon and keep hot. Pour the cooking juices into a saucepan and boil to reduce to a syrupy consistency, then pour over the chicory and serve.

Illustrated on PLATE 23

113

ETUVÉE DE CAROTTES AU CUMIN
Glazed Carrots Flavoured with Cumin

SERVES 4

450 g/1 lb carrots
a bunch of spring onions (scallions)
60 g/2 oz button mushrooms
60 g/2 oz/4 tablespoons unsalted butter
½ teaspoon ground cumin
½ teaspoon cumin seeds
1 clove of garlic
salt
½ tablespoon chopped fresh parsley

Peel and thinly slice the carrots; blanch them in boiling salted water for 1 minute, then drain. Trim and chop the spring onions; thinly slice the mushrooms.

Melt the butter in a sauté pan and add the carrots, ground cumin and cumin seeds. Cover and cook on a low heat for 15 minutes, stirring 3 or 4 times.

Put in the sliced mushrooms, spring onions, garlic crushed with the side of a knife, and 2 tablespoons of water. Add salt to taste and stir well to mix. Cook for a further 5 minutes, still covered.

Just before serving, add the chopped parsley.

BRUNO'S NOTES

The parsley can be replaced by fresh coriander (cilantro) leaves.

This is an excellent garnish with beef.

CRÊPES DE POMMES DE TERRE ET MAÏS
Sweetcorn and Potato Pancakes

SERVES 4

300 g/10 oz peeled potatoes
1 egg, separated
1 tablespoon cornflour (cornstarch)
1 tablespoon double cream (heavy cream)
salt and freshly ground black pepper
100 g/3½ oz/½ cup canned sweetcorn kernels
about 60 g/2 oz/4 tablespoons unsalted butter

Preheat the oven to 180°C/350°F/gas mark 4.
Cut the potatoes into chunks, then cook in boiling salted water until

soft – about 25 minutes depending on the quality of the potatoes. Drain in a colander and spread out in a roasting tin. Put into the oven to dry for 10 minutes.

Pass the potatoes through a mouli or potato ricer into a bowl. Add the egg yolk, cornflour and cream and mix together using a wooden spoon. Season with salt and pepper.

Drain the canned sweetcorn on paper towels, then add to the bowl and mix with the potato. Whisk the egg white with a tiny pinch of salt until stiff, and fold gently into the sweetcorn and potato mixture.

Melt a little butter in a non-stick frying pan. Spoon in enough of the sweetcorn mixture to shape 2 pancakes, each 8 cm/3 inches in diameter and 1 cm/½ inch thick. Cook on a low heat for 4 minutes on each side. Remove the pancakes from the pan and keep them hot while you make 6 more pancakes in the same way.

Serve hot.

RISOTTO AU SAFRAN
Saffron Risotto

SERVES 4

saffron threads
3½ tablespoons dry white wine
60 g/2 oz onion
3½ tablespoons olive oil
160 g/5½ oz/¾ cup risotto rice
1 clove of garlic
500 ml/16 fl oz Fond Blanc de Volaille (page 18)
30 g/1 oz/2 tablespoons unsalted butter
15 g/½ oz/2 tablespoons Parmesan cheese
freshly ground black pepper

PUT a pinch of saffron and the wine in a small cup and leave to soak for 10 minutes.

Meanwhile, peel and chop the onion. Heat the olive oil in a large saucepan and cook the onion for 2 minutes. Add the rice and cook for 1 minute, stirring with a wooden spatula. The rice will become shiny during this time.

Add the wine and saffron mixture and the finely chopped garlic and stir to mix. Cook until the rice has absorbed the wine, then add the chicken stock, one ladleful at a time. Stir frequently and wait for the rice to absorb the stock before adding the next ladleful.

When all the stock has been added and absorbed, which will take about 15 minutes, add the butter and the freshly grated Parmesan. Cook for a further 3 minutes, stirring frequently. When cooked, the rice should have a slightly firm yet creamy consistency. Season with pepper to taste, and serve.

OIGNONS AU FOUR AU GINGEMBRE
Roasted Onions with Ginger

SERVES 4

4 large onions, preferably sweet Italian ones
45 g/1½ oz fresh root ginger
4 cloves of garlic
100 g/3½ oz/7 tablespoons unsalted butter
salt and freshly ground black pepper
100 ml/3½ fl oz white wine vinegar
1 teaspoon coriander seeds

BRUNO'S NOTES

Check the onions from time to time during roasting, and add a little more water if the liquid in the tin has evaporated.

P REHEAT the oven to 180°C/350°F/gas mark 4. Peel the onions. Hollow out the centres with a knife to make a small hole. Peel the ginger and cut into fine *julienne*. Put a peeled clove of garlic and one-quarter of the ginger into the hole in each onion.

Place the onions in a small roasting tin. Cut the butter into 4 pieces and put one piece on each onion with some salt and pepper. Pour the vinegar into the tin and add 100 ml/3½ fl oz of water and the coriander seeds.

Put into the oven and roast for 1½ hours or until the onions are soft and caramelised, basting the onions with the juices in the tin. Serve hot.

FENOUIL BRAISÉ
Braised Fennel

SERVES 4

3½ tablespoons olive oil
4 small bulbs of fennel, or 2 very large ones cut in half
3½ tablespoons tarragon vinegar
2 cloves of garlic
1 star anise
500 ml/16 fl oz Fond Blanc de Volaille (page 18)
salt and freshly ground black pepper

H EAT the olive oil in a sauté pan, add the fennel and brown lightly on all sides. Deglaze the pan with the tarragon vinegar, stirring well, then add the garlic crushed with the side of a knife, the star anise and the chicken stock. Bring to the boil. Season very lightly with salt and pepper, then cover the pan and cook gently for 30 minutes or until the fennel is tender (test with the tip of a sharp knife).

Remove the fennel with a slotted spoon and keep hot. Boil the cooking juices until syrupy. To serve, pour the juices over the fennel.

CANELLONIS D'ÉPINARDS ET ARTICHAUTS
Spinach and Artichoke Canelloni

SERVES 4

100 g/3½ oz fresh spinach
2 globe artichokes
½ lemon
salt and freshly ground black pepper
2 slices of bread
6 tablespoons of milk
1 egg
2 cloves of garlic
250 g/9 oz Pâtes Fraîches (page 22)

BRUNO'S NOTES

These canelloni are an excellent accompaniment for a fish dish. They may also be served as a first course, sauced with melted butter and freshly grated Parmesan cheese, or as a vegetarian lunch dish for 2 or 3, with a tomato butter sauce and Parmesan.

REMOVE the stalks from the spinach and wash the leaves well. Blanch the leaves in boiling salted water until wilted, then drain and refresh in iced water. When cool enough to handle, squeeze the spinach in your hands to remove excess liquid. Chop the spinach roughly and set aside.

Cut the stalks off the globe artichokes with a sharp knife. Starting from the base, cut off all the leaves by turning the artichokes round, until you are left with just the bottoms or *fonds*. Put the bottoms into a pan of water. Squeeze the juice from the lemon half into the water and add the lemon half with 1 teaspoon of salt. Cut out a round of greaseproof or parchment paper to fit inside the pan, and cut a steam hole in the centre of the paper round. Place the paper on the water's surface. Bring to the boil, then simmer for 20 minutes or until the artichoke bottoms are tender (test with the tip of a sharp knife).

Drain the artichoke bottoms and remove the hairy chokes with a teaspoon or your thumb. Cut the bottoms into dice and set aside.

In a bowl, combine the bread, milk and egg, and mash them together with a fork. Add the chopped spinach, finely chopped garlic and diced artichokes and season to taste with salt and pepper.

On a lightly floured surface, roll out the pasta dough very thinly (about 1 mm). Cut out 8 squares, each about 10 × 10 cm/4 × 4 inches. Cook the pasta squares in boiling salted water for 2 minutes. Drain flat on a linen towel.

Place a piece of greased foil on the work surface. Lay one pasta square on top and put 2 tablespoons of the spinach and artichoke *farce* along the centre. Roll up to enclose the *farce*, using the foil to help lift the pasta. Wrap the canelloni in the foil, twisting the ends to seal. Repeat with the remaining pasta squares and *farce*.

Arrange the canelloni in a steamer, or stacked in a colander set in a large pan of boiling water, and cover. Steam for 5 minutes. Serve hot.

PURÉE D'HIVER
Purée of Winter Vegetables

SERVES 4

150 g/5 oz celeriac (celery root)
150 g/5 oz carrots
150 g/5 oz swede (rutabaga)
150 g/5 oz parsnips
salt
2 cloves of garlic
100 ml/3½ fl oz double cream (heavy cream)
60 g/2 oz/4 tablespoons unsalted butter
1 tablespoon chopped fresh chives

PEEL all the vegetables and cut them into small cubes. Put them in a large saucepan with a little salt and the garlic crushed with the side of a knife. Cover with water. Bring to the boil and simmer until all the vegetables are very tender.

Drain the vegetables well and pass them through a mouli or potato ricer to make a smooth purée.

Heat the cream with the butter in a pan until the butter has melted. Add the vegetable purée and chives and mix well with a wooden spoon. Serve hot.

BRUNO'S NOTES

You can use any combination of root vegetables you like for this purée. It works very well with game.

PETITS POIS À LA FRANÇAISE
Fresh Peas French-Style

SERVES 4

1.2 kg/2½ lb fresh peas
4 rashers of streaky bacon (slices of country-style bacon)
100 g/3½ oz onions
1 soft-leaved lettuce
salt and freshly ground black pepper
75 g/2½ oz/5 tablespoons unsalted butter
1 clove of garlic
a few sprigs of fresh thyme
100 ml/3½ fl oz dry white wine
a sprig of fresh flat-leaf parsley

SHELL the peas. Remove the rind from the bacon, if necessary, and cut the rashers across into fine *lardons*. Peel and chop the onions. Shred the lettuce into a *chiffonade*.

BRUNO'S NOTES

If you like, add a little salt to season, but remember that the bacon is salty.

Frozen green garden peas are as good if not better than fresh ones, and can be prepared this way. Choose the smallest ones, and thaw and drain them well, then add to the bacon mixture.

Bring a large pan of salted water to the boil. Add the peas to the boiling water and cook for about 5 minutes.

Meanwhile, melt 45 g/1½ oz/3 tablespoons of the butter in another large saucepan, add the bacon, chopped onions, finely chopped garlic and thyme and cook gently for 5 minutes, without colouring, stirring frequently. Stir in the lettuce *chiffonade*, then add the wine and bring to the boil.

Drain the peas and add to the bacon mixture. Cook for 5 minutes longer or until tender. Stir in the roughly chopped parsley. Add the remaining butter, cut in small pieces, and mix with a wooden spoon until it has melted. Season to taste with pepper, and serve.

PALETS À L'AIL
Potato and Garlic Cakes

SERVES 4

90 g/3 oz garlic
500 g/1 lb 2 oz potatoes
salt
1 egg
4 tablespoons flour
1 egg yolk
100 g/3½ oz/2 cups fine fresh breadcrumbs
1 tablespoon freshly grated Parmesan cheese
vegetable oil

BRUNO'S NOTES

Serve these with a roast shoulder of lamb or with roast duck.

P REHEAT the oven to 180°C/350°F/gas mark 4.
Peel the garlic cloves, then place them in a saucepan and add water to come 2 cm/¾ inch above the garlic. Cover the pan and simmer for about 30 minutes or until soft. Drain and set aside.

Peel the potatoes and cut them into chunks. Put them in a saucepan, cover with cold water and add ¾ teaspoon of salt. Bring to the boil and cook until soft – about 25 minutes depending on the quality of the potatoes.

Drain the potatoes in a colander, then spread them out in a roasting tin. Put into the oven to dry for 10 minutes.

Pass the potatoes through a mouli or potato ricer with the garlic into a bowl. Add the whole egg and mix well with a wooden spoon. With floured hands, shape the mixture into 12 small balls and flatten each one a little to obtain small hamburger shapes.

Prepare in front of you 4 plates: one with the flour, one with the egg yolk beaten with 3 tablespoons of water, one with the breadcrumbs mixed with the Parmesan, and one empty. Pass the potato cakes through the ingredient on each of the plates in the order given, to coat both sides, finishing on the empty plate. Chill for 30 minutes.

Heat a film of oil in a frying pan and fry the cakes for 5 minutes on each side or until golden brown. Or deep fry the cakes in hot oil. Serve hot.

Tranche de pain d'épices et chocolat blanc, sirop de prunes

Feuillantine de pommes à l'amande

Îles flottantes

Soufflé chaud au chocolat

Tatins de pommes à la verveine et romarin

Riz au lait de coco, glace au pain d'épices

Soufflé à la marmelade d'oranges

Poires pochées au cassis, glace au lait d'amandes

Mille feuille de chocolat aux cerises

Clafouti de cerises et pruneaux au chocolat

Crème brûlée au citron, gelée de citron

Gratin de pêches à la pistache

Gâteau de fromage blanc, 'punch' de fruits

Madeleines à la marmelade d'oranges

Brioche perdue et poire au gingembre

Tarte à la molasse

Tarte aux noix et figues sèches

Fruits pochés, biscuits au gingembre

Tuiles aux épices

Crème renversée au caramel

Salade de fruits éxotiques à l'anis et eau de rose

Figues confites à l'anis, parfait à la verveine

Coupe givrée moka

Pêches laquées aux épices

Salade de fruits rouges, glace au kümmel

Gelée de framboises et sorbet de melon charentais

CHAPTER SIX

Desserts

DESSERTS

I personally do not have a sweet tooth – maybe because I am fed up with the mousse and bavarois kind of dessert. Instead, here are some more modern recipes. Many might seem unusual, but in fact they are all based on classical or regional French desserts which I have adapted to my own taste.

TRANCHE DE PAIN D'ÉPICES ET CHOCOLAT BLANC, SIROP DE PRUNES

Iced Gingerbread and White Chocolate Terrine with Prunes in Syrup

SERVES ABOUT 12

800 ml/1⅓ pints/3¼ cups double cream (heavy cream)
300 g/10 oz white chocolate
50 g/1⅔ oz/3½ tablespoons unsalted butter
200 g/7 oz pain d'épices
450 g/1 lb/2¼ cups sugar
12 egg yolks
3½ tablespoons dark rum
2 tablespoons dark treacle or molasses
300 g/10 oz prunes
½ stick of cinnamon
500 ml/16 fl oz red wine
1½ tablespoons armagnac

BRUNO'S NOTES

This is a complicated recipe and it must be made in a large quantity. But you can slice what you need of the parfait and leave the rest in the freezer for another time, and the prunes can be kept for a week in the refrigerator.

BOIL 100 ml/3½ fl oz of the cream in a saucepan, then add the white chocolate, broken into small pieces, and the butter. Stir with a wooden spoon until completely melted and smooth. Remove from the heat and pour into a bowl. Chill, stirring from time to time, until the mixture is the thickness of mayonnaise.

Put the chocolate cream into a piping bag fitted with a large plain tube. Pipe on to a baking sheet lined with greaseproof or parchment paper to make 5 *boudins*, each 1 cm/½ inch in diameter and 28 cm/11 inches long. Place in the freezer to harden.

Combine the pain d'épices and 200 ml/7 fl oz of the cream, warmed, in a blender and process until very smooth. Put aside in the refrigerator.

Put 300 g/10 oz/1½ cups of the sugar and 250 ml/8 fl oz water in a saucepan. Bring to the boil, stirring just until the sugar has dissolved, then boil until the syrup reaches 108°C/226°F on a sugar thermometer. Remove the syrup from the heat and cool for 2 minutes, stirring constantly.

Put the egg yolks in a large bowl and slowly add the syrup, beating vigorously with a whisk. Continue whisking until the mixture is cold, then place in the refrigerator.

In another large bowl, whip the remaining cream until stiff. Pour the pain d'épices mixture and the egg yolk mixture over the cream and mix together with a pastry scraper. Return this parfait mixture to the refrigerator.

Line a 30 × 10 cm/12 × 4 inch terrine or loaf tin with dampened greaseproof or parchment paper, leaving it hanging over the sides of the mould.

Add the rum and treacle to the parfait mixture and mix quickly, then pour one-third into the mould. Place the mould in the freezer to harden for 20 minutes. Then place 2 of the white chocolate *boudins* on the layer of parfait in the mould and cover them with another third of the parfait mixture. Put back into the freezer for 20 minutes. Finally, arrange the remaining 3 chocolate *boudins* on the parfait in the mould and cover with the rest of the parfait mixture. Fold the paper over the top to cover the parfait and place in the freezer to set for about 6 hours.

Meanwhile, combine the prunes, cinnamon, red wine and remaining sugar in a saucepan. Bring to the boil and simmer for 30 minutes or until the liquid has a syrupy consistency. Leave to cool completely, then stir in the armagnac. Chill.

To serve, slice the moulded parfait and arrange as many slices as you like on the middle of each plate, then pour the prunes in syrup around.

Illustrated on PLATE 31

FEUILLANTINE DE POMMES À L'AMANDE
Puff Pastry Rounds Topped with Marzipan and Caramelised Apple

SERVES 4

200 g/7 oz puff pastry
4 Granny Smith apples
100 g/3½ oz marzipan
45 g/1½ oz/6 tablespoons icing sugar (confectioners' sugar)

BRUNO'S NOTES

You can serve this with a vanilla ice cream or even some whipped cream flavoured with vanilla or calvados.

ON a lightly floured surface, roll out the puff pastry until it is 2 mm/scant ⅛ inch thick. Using a 17 cm/7 inch plate or pastry cutter as a guide, cut out 4 rounds. Place the rounds in the refrigerator to rest.

Meanwhile, peel the apples, cut them in half and remove the core. Slice each half thinly.

Cut the marzipan into quarters and roll out each piece to a round 12 cm/5 inches in diameter.

Preheat the oven to 220°C/425°F/gas mark 7.

Take the puff pastry rounds out of the refrigerator and place them on a lightly floured baking tray or a baking tray lined with parchment paper. With a knife, mark a ring inside each round, 5 mm/¼ inch in from the edge (this outside edge will rise during baking to make a rim). Prick the centres of the rounds with a fork (don't prick the outside ring).

Place a round of marzipan in the centre of each round of pastry and arrange the apple slices on the marzipan. Place in the oven and bake for about 20 minutes.

Sift the icing sugar over the apples and bake for a further 5 minutes. When ready, the pastry rim will be risen and golden brown and the apples tender and glazed.

Serve warm.

ÎLES FLOTTANTES
Floating Islands

SERVES 4

MERINGUE
6 egg whites
salt
300 g/10 oz/1½ cups caster sugar (superfine sugar)

FOR POACHING
1 litre/1¾ pints/1 quart milk
1 vanilla pod (vanilla bean)

CREAM
100 g/3½ oz/½ cup caster sugar (U.S. granulated sugar)
12 egg yolks
about 2 tablespoons dark rum or kirsch or even a few drops of pastis
(optional)

TO FINISH
45 g/1½ oz/½ cup toasted flaked almonds (sliced almonds)
100 g/3½ oz/½ cup caster sugar (U.S. granulated sugar)
lemon juice

TO make the meringue, in a large, clean stainless steel or glass bowl, whisk the egg whites with a tiny pinch of salt to a soft peak. Gradually add the sugar and continue whisking until the meringue is stiff.

Put the milk in a large, wide heavy-based pan. Split open the vanilla pod and add to the milk. Bring to the boil, then reduce the heat until the milk is just simmering. Dip two tablespoons in warm water and use them to shape half of the meringue mixture into 2 *quenelles*. Poach the meringues in the simmering milk for 2 minutes on each side. Remove them with a slotted spoon and put them aside on a tray. Repeat the operation with the remaining meringue mixture. Set the 4 meringues aside while you make the cream.

In a bowl, whisk together the sugar and egg yolks until very smooth and white. Pour over the hot poaching milk, whisking well. Pour the mixture back into the milk saucepan and cook over a low heat, stirring constantly with a wooden spoon, until the cream thickens enough to coat the spoon. Strain quickly into a large, deep serving dish. Leave to cool, then gently stir in the rum, kirsch or pastis. Cover and chill.

When ready to serve, top the cream with the poached meringues and sprinkle over the almonds. In a small saucepan, melt the sugar with 2 tablespoons of water and a drop of lemon juice. When the sugar turns a caramel colour, pour it quickly over the meringues.

SOUFFLÉ CHAUD AU CHOCOLAT
Hot Chocolate Soufflé

BRUNO'S NOTES

There are so many different ways to make a chocolate soufflé. I chose this one because it is the simplest and quickest to prepare. If you like, serve the soufflés with an ice cream of your choice or simply with a Crème Anglaise (page 25).

SERVES 4

½ orange
8 egg yolks
70 g/2⅓ oz/⅓ cup caster sugar (superfine sugar)
50 g/1⅔ oz/9 tablespoons unsweetened cocoa powder
2 tablespoons whisky
12 egg whites
salt
unsweetened cocoa powder

FOR THE DISHES
50 g/1⅔ oz/3½ tablespoons unsalted butter, at room temperature
50 g/1⅔ oz/¼ cup caster sugar (U.S. granulated sugar)

WITH your finger, evenly butter the inside of 4 individual soufflé dishes, each 10 cm/4 inches in diameter and 5 cm/2 inches high. Put the sugar into one of the dishes and rotate it to coat all the surface. Tip all the excess sugar into another dish and rotate to coat it. Repeat until you have sugared all 4 dishes. Set aside.

Very finely pare the zest from the orange half, taking none of the white pith, then chop the zest as finely as possible. Blanch in boiling water for 1 minute; drain and dry on paper towels. (Use the orange flesh in another dish.)

Preheat the oven to 200°C/400°F/gas mark 6.

In a bowl, whisk together the egg yolks and 50 g/1⅔ oz/¼ cup of the sugar until very smooth and white. Add the cocoa powder, whisky and orange zest and mix well.

In a large, clean stainless steel or glass bowl, whisk the egg whites with a tiny pinch of salt to a soft peak. Add the remaining sugar and continue whisking until the mixture becomes firm but not too stiff.

Add one-quarter of the egg whites to the egg yolk mixture and mix together with a whisk, then fold in the remaining egg whites. (This operation is easy if you use a pastry scraper.)

Fill the prepared soufflé dishes with the mixture, right to the top and then above the rim by about 1 cm/½ inch. Be careful not to get any of the mixture on the edges of the dishes or the soufflés will stick to the dishes and will not rise evenly.

Set the dishes in a roasting tin and add enough hot water to the tin to come 1 cm/½ inch up the sides of the dishes. Place the tin on top of the stove and bring the water to the boil, then transfer to the oven. Bake for about 12 minutes, reducing the temperature to 190°C/375°F/gas mark 5 as soon as the soufflés start to rise.

When the soufflés are puffed up, remove them from their *bain-marie* of hot water, quickly dry the dishes and place on plates. Sprinkle some cocoa powder over the soufflés through a sieve and serve immediately.

TATINS DE POMMES À LA VERVEINE ET ROMARIN

Apple Tarts Flavoured with Strega and Rosemary

SERVES 4

6 Granny Smith apples
60 g/2 oz/4 tablespoons unsalted butter
45 g/1½ oz/4½ tablespoons soft light brown sugar
1½ tablespoons Strega liqueur or Verveine du Velay liqueur
a branch of fresh rosemary
¼ cinnamon stick
¼ vanilla pod (vanilla bean)
sprigs of fresh rosemary to decorate

PASTRY
125 g/4⅓ oz/¾ cup flour
45 g/1½ oz/6 tablespoons icing sugar (confectioners' sugar)
finely grated zest of 1 lemon
a pinch of salt
100 g/3½ oz/7 tablespoons unsalted butter, at room temperature
1 egg yolk

FIRST make the pastry. Put all the ingredients into a food processor and process for 10 seconds or just until a dough is formed around the blades. Turn out the dough on to a lightly floured work surface and work with the palms of your hands until smooth. Wrap and chill for at least 30 minutes.

Meanwhile, peel the apples, cut them in half and remove the cores. Cut each half into 4 wedges. In a large frying pan, melt the butter, add the apples and fry them for 3 minutes, stirring frequently. Sprinkle over the brown sugar and fry for a further 2 minutes, stirring gently. At this stage, the sugar on the apples should be slightly caramelised. Deglaze the pan with the liqueur, stirring well, and add the very finely chopped rosemary leaves, the cinnamon stick and vanilla pod. Remove from the heat and leave to infuse and cool. When the apples are cold, drain them, reserving the syrup. Strain the syrup into a small pan and set aside.

Preheat the oven to 220°C/425°F/gas mark 7.

Arrange the apple wedges in four 10–12 cm/4–5 inch diameter tartlet moulds, preferably with removable bottoms. On a lightly floured work surface, roll out the dough to 2 mm/scant ⅛ inch thick. Cut out 4 rounds slightly bigger than the tartlet moulds. Lay a round over each mould and, with the back of a knife blade, gently ease the edge of the dough down between the apples and the mould. Make a small hole in the centre of each pastry lid so that the steam can escape during baking.

Set the moulds on a baking sheet and bake in the hot oven for 6–8 minutes or until the pastry is golden brown. While the tarts are baking, reheat the syrup. Turn out the tarts, upside-down, on hot plates. Spoon round the syrup and decorate with rosemary sprigs. Serve immediately.

BRUNO'S NOTES

The liqueur and rosemary in this version of the classic Tarte Tatin make this superb dessert even more flavourful.

RIZ AU LAIT DE COCO, GLACE AU PAIN D'ÉPICES

Coconut Rice Pudding with Gingerbread Ice Cream

SERVES 4

50 g/1⅔ oz/¼ cup pudding rice (short-grain rice)
250 ml/8 fl oz canned unsweetened coconut milk
100 ml/3½ fl oz milk
a strip of orange zest
25 g/¾ oz/2 tablespoons caster sugar (U.S. granulated sugar)
½ vanilla pod (vanilla bean)
100 ml/3½ fl oz double cream (heavy cream)
2 tablespoons Malibu or other coconut and rum cream liqueur

ICE CREAM
500 ml/16 fl oz Crème Anglaise (page 25)
150 g/5 oz pain d'épices
2 tablespoons dark treacle or molasses
1 tablespoon dark rum
50 g/1⅔ oz candied orange peel

BRUNO'S NOTES

You will probably have some ice cream left over, but it will keep very well in the freezer for 2–3 days. If stored in the freezer, the ice cream will be very hard, so soften it for serving by scraping it with a spoon dipped occasionally into hot water until it is moist but not melted.

PUT the rice in a saucepan, cover with cold water and bring to the boil. Drain and rinse under cold running water.

In a heavy saucepan, combine the coconut milk, milk, orange zest, sugar and vanilla pod. Bring to the boil, then add the rice and stir to mix. Reduce the heat to very low, put a lid on the pan and leave to cook very gently at just simmering point for about 1 hour, stirring from time to time.

When the rice mixture is cooked, remove from the heat and leave to cool with the lid on. When the mixture is cold, remove the vanilla pod and orange zest, and stir in the cream and Malibu. Pour into a bowl, cover and chill.

To make the ice cream, mix together the crème anglaise, diced pain d'épices, treacle and rum. Finely dice the candied orange peel and mix it in. Pour into an electric ice cream machine and churn until softly set.

To serve, spoon the rice pudding into soup plates and top each serving with a large scoop of ice cream. Decorate according to your taste with unsweetened cocoa powder or shavings of fresh coconut.

BRIOCHE PERDUE ET POIRE AU GINGEMBRE

Pan-Fried Brioche and Pear with Ginger

SERVES 4

2 large ripe pears, preferably William's (Bartlett)
120 g/4 oz/1½ cup + 2 tablespoons sugar
juice of ½ lemon
½ vanilla pod (vanilla bean)
15 g/½ oz fresh root ginger
60 g/2 oz/3 tablespooons clear honey
200 ml/7 fl oz double cream (heavy cream)
dark rum
1 egg
100 ml/3½ fl oz milk
4 slices of brioche, each 2 cm/¾ inch thick
small piece of unsalted butter
200 ml/7 fl oz Crème Anglaise (page 25)

PEEL the pears, cut them in half lengthways and remove the cores. Put them in a saucepan with 100 g/3½ oz/½ cup of the sugar, the lemon juice and the vanilla pod. Just cover with water and put a lid on the pan. Bring to simmering point and cook gently for about 10 minutes or until the pears are just tender. (The cooking time of the pears can vary according to the quality of the fruit.) Remove from the heat and leave to cool in the syrup.

Put the remaining sugar in a small pan. Peel and chop the ginger and add to the pan with 1 tablespoon of water. Heat until the sugar has melted and turned to a nice golden caramel. Add the honey and cream and cook gently for a further 5 minutes, stirring frequently, until the caramel has dissolved in the cream. Strain through a very fine sieve into a bowl. Stir in a few drops of rum, and put aside.

In a soup plate, mix together the egg and milk. Dip both sides of the brioche slices in this mixture to soak them. Pan-fry the brioche in butter until golden brown on both sides.

To serve, place a slice of brioche on the middle of each plate with a drained pear half. Pour the crème anglaise around, and spoon the gingered caramel sauce over the pears.

Illustrated opposite

Brioche Perdue et Poire au Gingembre

Pan-Fried Brioche and Pear with Ginger

PLATE 25

Clafouti de Cerises et Pruneaux au Chocolat

Clafouti of Cherries and Prunes with Chocolate
(recipe page 131)

PLATE 26

Poire Pochée au Cassis, Glace au Lait d'Amandes

Poached Pear with Blackcurrants and Almond Ice Cream
(recipe page 137)

PLATE 27

Gelée de Framboises et Sorbet de Melon Charentais

Fresh Raspberry Jelly and Melon Sorbet
(recipe page 145)

PLATE 28

Crème Brûlée au Citron, Gelée de Citron

Lemon Crème Brûlée with a Fresh Lemon Jelly
(recipe page 132)

PLATE 29

Mille Feuille de Chocolat aux Cerises

———————

Chocolate and Cherry Mille Feuille
(recipe page 130)

PLATE 30

Tranche de Pain d'Épices et Chocolat Blanc, Sirop de Prunes

Iced Gingerbread and White Chocolate Terrine with Prunes in Syrup
(recipe page 122)

PLATE 31

Salade de Fruits Éxotiques à l'Anis et Eau de Rose

Salad of Exotic Fruits Flavoured with Star Anise and Rosewater
(recipe page 141)

PLATE 32

TARTE À LA MOLASSE
Molasses or Dark Treacle Tart

SERVES 4

PASTRY
125 g/4⅓ oz/¾ cup flour
60 g/2 oz/4 tablespoons unsalted butter, at room temperature
1 teaspoon caster sugar (superfine sugar)
1 egg
1 egg yolk

FILLING
3 eggs
1 egg yolk
150 ml/5 fl oz double cream (heavy cream)
100 ml/3½ fl oz molasses or dark treacle
75 g/2½ oz/½ cup sultanas (golden raisins)
freshly grated nutmeg
icing sugar (confectioners' sugar)

TO make the pastry, put all the ingredients and 1½ tablespoons of cold water into a food processor and process for 10 seconds or just until a dough is formed around the blades. Turn out on to the work surface. With the palms of your hands, work the dough briefly until smooth. Wrap and leave to rest in the refrigerator for at least 30 minutes.

Roll out the dough on a lightly floured work surface until it is 3 mm/⅛ inch thick. Use to line an 18 cm/7½ inch loose-bottomed tart tin, gently easing the dough in. Cut off the excess dough around the rim, leaving a 1.5 cm/scant ¾ inch overhang. Tuck this overhang under all around the rim so that the edge of the pastry case rises above the rim of the tin. Flute the edge and prick the bottom of the pastry case with a fork. Place in the refrigerator to rest for 15 minutes.

Preheat the oven to 190°C/375°F/gas mark 5. Place a baking sheet in the oven to heat.

Line the pastry case with greaseproof or parchment paper and fill it with baking beans. Place the tin on the baking sheet in the oven and bake for 10 minutes, then remove the paper and beans and bake for a further 5 minutes.

Remove the pastry case from the oven and set it aside to cool slightly. Reduce the oven temperature to 180°C/350°F/gas mark 4.

Put the whole eggs, egg yolk, cream, molasses or treacle, sultanas and a pinch of nutmeg in a bowl and mix together. Pour the filling into the pastry case. Bake for 30 minutes or until set.

Sprinkle some sifted icing sugar over the filling. Protect the edge of the pastry case with foil, and glaze the sugar topping under the grill (broiler). Serve the tart warm.

MILLE FEUILLE DE CHOCOLAT AUX CERISES
Chocolate and Cherry Mille Feuille

SERVES 4

350 g/12 oz best-quality plain or semisweet chocolate (chocolat pâtissier)
150 g/5 oz best-quality bittersweet chocolate
20 g/²⁄₃ oz/1½ tablespoons unsalted butter
200 g/7 oz/1 cup + 3 tablespoons caster sugar (superfine sugar)
3 eggs, separated
salt
4 tablespoons whipping cream
250 g/9 oz/1 pint fresh black cherries
300 ml/10 fl oz Crème Anglaise (page 25)
1 tablespoon unsweetened cocoa powder

FIRST make the chocolate layers. Put the plain or semisweet chocolate in a heatproof bowl and set it in a pan of hot water. Stir until the chocolate is melted and smooth, then remove the bowl from the *bain-marie* of hot water.

Lay 1 or 2 perfectly clean, cut open plastic file folders (from a stationers) on a very flat tray, making sure there are no air bubbles. Spread the melted chocolate over the plastic file as thinly as possible using a rubber spatula. Leave in a cool place until almost set. Before the chocolate is completely hard, cut it with a pastry cutter or knife to make 12 rectangles, each 9 × 4 cm/3¾ × 1¾ inches. Leave to set completely on the plastic in a cool place (not the refrigerator).

Meanwhile, put the bittersweet chocolate and butter in a large heatproof bowl and set it in the *bain-marie*. Stir until melted and smooth, then stir in 1 tablespoon of the sugar until dissolved. Remove the bowl from the *bain-marie*. Incorporate the egg yolks, one by one.

Whisk the egg whites with a tiny pinch of salt until stiff, then whisk in 2 tablespoons of the remaining sugar. Whip the cream until stiff but not buttery. Fold the cream and egg whites gently but thoroughly into the chocolate mixture using a large spoon. Put into the refrigerator to set.

While the mousse is chilling, poach the cherries. Using a cherry pitter, remove the cherry stones. Put the remaining sugar in a saucepan with 500 ml/16 fl oz of water and bring to a simmer, stirring occasionally to dissolve the sugar. Add the cherries to the syrup and cook gently for 5 minutes. Remove from the heat and leave the cherries to cool in the syrup.

The chocolate leaves should now be hard. Peel them carefully from the plastic, handling them as little as possible.

Spoon the chocolate mousse into a piping bag fitted with a 1.25 cm/½ inch tube. Drain the cherries.

Pipe a little spot of mousse in the centre of each plate and place a

BRUNO'S NOTES

You can spread the melted chocolate on a sheet of parchment paper rather than the plastic file, but your chocolate leaves will not have the same shine.

For a chocolate and mint 'mille feuille', you can replace the cherries with sweetened whipped cream flavoured with mint essence (mint extract).

Any chocolate trimmings can be used in other desserts. The cherry syrup can be stored in a jar in the refrigerator and used again, to poach red fruits for example.

chocolate rectangle on top. Pipe 3 spots of mousse on the long sides of each rectangle, and place a cherry between each spot. Put another chocolate rectangle on top, and repeat the operation. Finish with a chocolate rectangle. Pour the crème anglaise around each 'mille feuille'. Sprinkle over a little cocoa powder through a sieve, and serve.

Illustrated on PLATE 30

CLAFOUTI DE CERISES ET PRUNEAUX AU CHOCOLAT
Clafouti of Cherries and Prunes with Chocolate

SERVES 4

300 g/10 oz prunes
300 g/10 oz sweet cherries (fresh or canned)
60 g/2 oz/²⁄₃ cup ground almonds
1 tablespoon cornflour (cornstarch)
100 g/3½ oz/½ cup caster sugar (U.S. granulated sugar)
salt
20 g/²⁄₃ oz/¼ cup unsweetened cocoa powder
2 eggs
1 egg yolk
30 g/1 oz/2 tablespoons unsalted butter
2 tablespoons double cream (heavy cream)
3 tablespoons armagnac
icing sugar (confectioners' sugar)

BRUNO'S NOTES

You can also use the prune and cherry mixture as the filling for a *pâte sablée* tart, but bake the pastry case blind for 10 minutes first.

PUT the prunes in a bowl of hot water and leave to soak for 2 hours. Drain and remove the stones. If using canned cherries, drain them.
Preheat the oven to 180°C/350°F/gas mark 4.
In a large bowl, combine the ground almonds, cornflour, sugar, a pinch of salt, cocoa powder, whole eggs and egg yolk. Mix everything together well with a wooden spoon.
Put the butter in a small pan and heat until it has melted and turned a light brown (*noisette*). Pour it quickly into a small bowl and cool slightly, then add to the almond mixture with the cream and armagnac. Mix well.
Stir the prunes and cherries into the almond mixture. Pour into individual ramekin dishes or one large gratin dish. Set the dishes in a roasting tin and add hot water to the tin to come halfway up the sides of the ramekins. Bake for about 10 minutes.
Increase the oven heat to 190°C/375°F/gas mark 5, and bake for 5 minutes longer or until set and lightly browned.
Remove the ramekins from the *bain-marie* of hot water and cool slightly, then dredge with sifted icing sugar and serve warm with an ice cream of your choice.

Illustrated on PLATE 26

CRÈME BRÛLÉE AU CITRON, GELÉE DE CITRON

Lemon Crème Brûlée with a Fresh Lemon Jelly

SERVES 4

CRÈME BRÛLÉE
3 egg yolks
150 g/5 oz/³⁄₄ cup caster sugar (U.S. granulated sugar)
2 eggs
juice of 3 lemons
juice of 1 orange
150 ml/5 fl oz double cream (heavy cream)
80 g/2²⁄₃ oz/¹⁄₂ cup light brown sugar

JELLY
1 leaf of gelatine
1 lemon
50 g/1²⁄₃ oz/¹⁄₄ cup caster sugar (U.S. granulated sugar)
50 g/1²⁄₃ oz best-quality bittersweet chocolate

BRUNO'S NOTES

For a long time I have had this crème on my menu, with a jasmine tea sorbet.

PREHEAT the oven to 180°C/350°F/gas mark 4.
First make the crèmes brûlées. In a bowl, whisk together the egg yolks and white sugar until very smooth and white. Add the whole eggs and the lemon and orange juices. Bring the cream to the boil in a small pan, then whisk it into the egg mixture.

Pour the mixture into 4 ramekin dishes. Set the dishes in a roasting tin and add enough hot water to the tin to come 1 cm/¹⁄₂ inch up the sides of the dishes. Place in the oven and bake for about 30 minutes or until the creams are set – touch the surface with your finger: it should not feel sticky.

In the meantime, prepare the lemon jelly. Soak the leaf of gelatine in cold water to soften it. Pare the zest from the lemon and squeeze out the juice. Combine 100 ml/3¹⁄₂ fl oz of water with the sugar and lemon zest in a saucepan and bring to the boil. Boil for 5 minutes, then add the lemon juice and boil for 30 seconds longer. Remove from the heat. Squeeze dry the leaf of gelatine, then add it to the lemon mixture and stir until completely dissolved. Set aside to cool, then strain to remove the lemon zest.

When the crèmes brûlées are cooked, lift them out of the *bain-marie* of hot water and set them in a tray filled with iced water. Leave to cool completely.

Put the chocolate in a small heatproof bowl and set it in the *bain-marie*. Stir until the chocolate is melted and smooth. Put the chocolate into a greaseproof or parchment paper piping cone and snip off the tip to make a tiny hole (or use a piping bag fitted with a fine writing tube). Pipe the chocolate in a triangular shape on the centre of each plate. Leave to set.

When the chocolate has set, carefully pour the lemon jelly around the outside of each chocolate triangle. Leave to set in the refrigerator.

With a thin knife blade, loosen the crèmes brûlées from the ramekins and turn them out upside-down on to a baking sheet. Cover the tops of the crèmes evenly with the brown sugar. Place under a hot grill (broiler) to melt and caramelise the sugar.

Carefully transfer the crèmes brûlées to the plates, placing them in the centre of the chocolate triangles.

Illustrated on PLATE 29

GRATIN DE PÊCHES À LA PISTACHE
Caramelised Peaches with Pistachio Cream

SERVES 4

8 medium-sized ripe but firm peaches
juice of 1 lime
2 eggs
100 g/3½ oz/½ cup caster sugar (U.S. granulated sugar)
25 g/¾ oz/2½ tablespoons flour
250 ml/8 fl oz hot milk
100 g/3½ oz shelled and peeled pistachios
30 g/1 oz/2 tablespoons unsalted butter
almond essence (almond extract)
2 egg whites
salt
4 teaspoons demerara sugar (raw brown sugar)

BRUNO'S NOTES

To remove the skins from pistachios, blanch them in boiling water for 3 minutes, then drain and rinse under cold running water. Rub them gently in a linen towel, and the skins will slip off easily.

BRING a large pot of water to the boil. Drop the peaches into the water and blanch for 2 minutes, then lift them into a bowl of iced water. Drain the peaches and slip off their skins.

Cut 2 of the peaches in half and remove the stones. Put the peaches in a blender and work to obtain a smooth *coulis*. Mix the lime juice into the *coulis*. Set aside.

Cut the remaining peaches into small wedges and use to cover the bottoms of 4 individual gratin dishes. Set aside.

In a bowl, whisk the eggs with half of the sugar until well mixed, then add the flour and hot milk. Pour into a saucepan and cook on a very low heat for 20 minutes or until quite thick, stirring from time to time with a wooden spoon. Pour this cream into the blender and add the pistachios, butter and a drop or so of almond essence to taste. Work until well combined and smooth. Transfer to a large bowl and set aside at room temperature.

In another large bowl, whisk the egg whites with a very tiny pinch of salt until stiff. Whisk in the remaining sugar. Fold the egg whites gently but thoroughly into the pistachio cream, using a large spoon.

Pour the pistachio cream over the peaches in the gratin dishes and smooth the tops. Sprinkle over the demerara sugar. Put the dishes under a preheated low grill (broiler) for 5 minutes, then turn the heat up to high, or move the dish closer to the source of heat, to caramelise the sugar.

Serve with the peach *coulis* as a sauce.

GÂTEAU DE FROMAGE BLANC, 'PUNCH' DE FRUITS
Pineapple Cheesecake with a Fruit 'Punch'

SERVES 4

100 g/3½ oz wholewheat digestive biscuits (7 whole large rectangular graham crackers)
50 g/1⅔ oz/3½ tablespoons unsalted butter, melted
50 g/1⅔ oz/3½ tablespoons full fat soft cheese
75 ml/2½ fl oz sour cream
120 g/4 oz/½ cup cottage cheese
2 leaves of gelatine
250 ml/8 fl oz liquidised fresh pineapple flesh
3½ tablespoons Malibu or other coconut and rum cream liqueur
2 egg whites
salt
50 g/1⅔ oz/¼ cup caster sugar (superfine sugar)

PUNCH
100 ml/3½ fl oz red wine
50 g/1⅔ oz/¼ cup sugar
½ stick of cinnamon
1 peach
1 orange
100 g/3½ oz/¾ cup raspberries

FINELY crush the digestive biscuits, then mix with the melted butter. Press the mixture evenly over the bottom of a 22 cm/9 inch springform cake tin and refrigerate until set.

Meanwhile, put the soft cheese, sour cream and cottage cheese into a blender and work until smooth. Put aside in a large bowl. Soak the gelatine leaves in cold water to soften them.

In a small pan, bring the pineapple pulp to the boil. Remove from the heat. Squeeze the gelatine and add it to the pineapple pulp in the pan. Stir until the gelatine has dissolved. Chill the mixture until it is completely cold.

Add the cheese mixture and the Malibu to the pineapple mixture and stir together thoroughly with a wooden spoon. Whisk the egg whites with a tiny pinch of salt to a soft peak. Add the sugar and continue whisking until stiff. Fold the egg whites into the pineapple mixture. Pour the mixture into the cake tin on top of the biscuit base. Cover and chill until the filling is set.

To make the punch, in a small saucepan boil the red wine with the sugar and cinnamon for 5 minutes. Remove from the heat and stir in 100 ml/3½ fl oz of water. Pour into a bowl.

Peel, stone and dice the peach. Peel the orange and divide into segments, cutting down between the dividing membranes. Lightly crush the raspberries. Add all these fruits to the wine syrup and stir gently. Cover and chill.

To serve, slice the cheesecake, put on plates and pour the punch around.

MADELEINES À LA MARMELADE D'ORANGES
Madeleines with White Chocolate and Orange Marmalade

MAKES 24 (12 pairs)

50 g/1²/₃ oz/3¹/₂ tablespoons unsalted butter
50 g/1²/₃ oz/6¹/₂ tablespoons icing sugar (confectioners' sugar)
20 g/²/₃ oz/2 tablespoons self-raising flour (self-rising flour)
20 g/²/₃ oz/¹/₄ cup ground almonds
bicarbonate of soda (baking soda)
finely grated zest of ¹/₄ orange
1¹/₂ egg whites
2 teaspoons clear honey
250 g/9 oz white chocolate
100 g/3¹/₂ oz/¹/₃ cup orange marmalade

BRUNO'S NOTES

These little cakes are very nice with coffee or afternoon tea. Take care not to overcook them as they should be moist.

PUT the butter in a small pan and heat until it has melted and turned a light brown (*noisette*). Pour it quickly into a small bowl and leave to cool slightly.

In a large bowl, mix together the sugar, flour, ground almonds, 2 pinches of bicarbonate of soda and the orange zest. Add the egg whites and mix in very well using a spoon. Finally, add the butter and honey and mix to obtain a smooth and quite liquid paste. Chill for at least 30 minutes.

Preheat the oven to 170°C/325°F/gas mark 3.

Stir the paste to be sure it is well mixed, then put it into a piping bag fitted with a large plain tube. Grease madeleine moulds with butter and pipe in the paste to fill them.

Place the moulds in the oven and bake for about 15 minutes or until slightly risen and light golden brown. Cool slightly in the moulds, then turn out on to a wire rack.

Put the chocolate in a heatproof bowl and set it in a pan of hot water. Stir until the chocolate is melted and smooth. Dip half of the madeleines, one by one, in the melted chocolate, holding them between two fingers. Coat two-thirds of each madeleine with chocolate. Place them on a tray lined with greaseproof or waxed paper and leave to set in a cool place.

Sandwich together the chocolate-coated madeleines and the plain madeleines, sticking the pairs together with the marmalade.

SOUFFLÉ À LA MARMELADE D'ORANGES
Orange Marmalade Soufflé

SERVES 4

8 egg whites
salt
40 g/1⅓ oz/3½ tablespoons caster sugar (superfine sugar)
2 tablespoons Grand Marnier
4 tablespoons orange marmalade

FOR THE DISHES
50 g/1⅔ oz/3½ tablespoons unsalted butter, softened
50 g/1⅔ oz/¼ cup caster sugar (U.S. granulated sugar)

CRÈME PÂTISSIÈRE
250 ml/8 fl oz milk
a strip of orange zest
5 egg yolks
50 g/1⅔ oz/¼ cup caster sugar (U.S. granulated sugar)
30 g/1 oz/3 tablespoons flour
10 g/⅓ oz/2 teaspoons unsalted butter
icing sugar (confectioners' sugar)

BRUNO'S NOTES

If the soufflés appear to be sticking to the edges of the dishes when they start to rise, free them with a knife.

When folding in the egg whites, do not overmix and lose all the air beaten into the whites, or the soufflés will not rise. It is all right if bits of white can still be seen in the crème pâtissière.

WITH your finger, evenly butter the inside of 4 individual soufflé dishes, each 10 cm/4 inches in diameter and 5 cm/2 inches deep. Put the sugar in one of the dishes and rotate it to coat all the surface, then tip the excess sugar into a second dish and rotate to coat it. Repeat until you have sugared all the dishes. Set them aside.

To make the crème pâtissière, combine the milk and orange zest in a heavy-based saucepan and bring to the boil. Meanwhile, in a bowl, whisk together 3 of the egg yolks and the sugar until very smooth and white. Add the flour. Pour half the boiling milk over the egg yolk mixture, whisking well, then pour back into the pan. Bring back to the boil, whisking constantly, and cook until the mixture becomes thick. Then turn the heat very low and cook for about 15 minutes, stirring with a wooden spoon.

Pour the crème pâtissière into a large bowl. Discard the orange zest, and mix in the remaining 2 egg yolks. Add the butter and mix well, then sprinkle some sifted icing sugar over the surface. Set aside to cool.

Preheat the oven to 200°C/400°F/gas mark 6.

In a large, clean stainless steel or glass bowl, whisk the egg whites with a tiny pinch of salt to a soft peak. Add the sugar and continue whisking until the mixture is firm but not too stiff: it should hold its shape on the whisk when lifted out. Add one-quarter of the egg whites to the crème pâtissière and mix together with the whisk, then fold in the remaining egg whites and the Grand Marnier. (This operation is easy if you use a plastic pastry scraper.)

Half fill each soufflé dish with the mixture, then put a tablespoon of marmalade in the centre. Add the rest of the mixture, to fill the dishes right to the top and then above the rim by about 1 cm/½ inch. Be careful not to get any of the mixture on the edges of the dishes or the soufflés will not rise evenly.

Set the dishes in a roasting tin and add enough hot water to the tin to come 1 cm/½ inch up the sides of the dishes. Place the tin on top of the stove and bring the water to the boil, then transfer to the oven. Bake for about 12 minutes, reducing the temperature to 190°C/375°F/gas mark 5 as soon as the soufflés start to rise.

When the soufflés are puffed up and lightly golden, remove them from their *bain-marie* of hot water, quickly dry the dishes and place on plates. Sift over a little icing sugar and serve immediately.

POIRES POCHÉES AU CASSIS, GLACE AU LAIT D'AMANDES

Poached Pears with Blackcurrants and Almond Ice Cream

SERVES 4

4 large ripe pears, preferably William's (Bartlett)
200 g/7 oz/1⅓ cups frozen blackcurrants, or mixture of frozen red fruits
100 g/3½ oz/½ cup caster sugar (U.S. granulated sugar)
300 ml/10 fl oz Crème Anglaise (page 25)
200 ml/7 fl oz double cream (heavy cream)
almond essence (almond extract)
2 tablespoons kirsch (optional)
sprigs of fresh mint to decorate

PEEL the pears. Put them in a saucepan with the blackcurrants, sugar and 500 ml/16 fl oz of water. Cover the pan. Bring to simmering point and cook gently for about 10 minutes or until the pears are just tender.

Remove the pears with a slotted spoon and place them in a bowl. Press the blackcurrant sauce through a fine sieve on to the pears. Leave to cool completely.

Mix the crème anglaise and cream together and flavour to taste with a few drops of almond essence and the kirsch.

Churn the mixture in an electric ice cream machine for about 15 minutes or until softly set.

To serve, place a pear on one side of each soup plate and spoon the blackcurrant sauce round them. Add 2 *quenelles* of almond ice cream to each plate and garnish with a sprig of sugared mint.

Illustrated on PLATE 27

TARTE AUX NOIX ET FIGUES SÈCHES
Walnut and Fig Tart

SERVES 4-6

PASTRY
125 g/4⅓ oz/¾ cup flour
100 g/3½ oz/7 tablespoons unsalted butter, at room temperature
1 egg yolk
salt

FILLING
75 g/2½ oz dried figs
200 g/7 oz/7-8 slices white bread
100 g/3½ oz/5 tablespoons dark treacle or molasses
100 g/3½ oz/5 tablespoons golden syrup (light corn syrup)
60 g/2 oz shelled walnuts
juice of ½ lemon

IN a food processor, combine the flour, butter, egg yolk, a pinch of salt and 1 tablespoon of water. Process for 10 seconds or just until a dough is formed around the blades. Turn the dough out on to the work surface and briefly work it with the palms of the hands until smooth. Wrap the dough and chill for at least 30 minutes.

Meanwhile, place the figs in a small saucepan, cover with cold water and bring to the boil. Simmer for 10 minutes. Drain the figs and cut them into 5 mm/¼ inch cubes. Put aside.

Preheat the oven to 220°C/425°F/gas mark 7.

In the food processor, combine the bread, treacle or molasses, golden syrup, walnuts and lemon juice. Process for 1 minute. Tip the mixture into a bowl and mix in the figs.

On a lightly floured surface, roll out the dough to 4 mm/scant ¼ inch thick and use to line a 20–22 cm/8–9 inch loose-bottomed tart tin, gently easing the dough in. Cut off the excess dough around the rim, leaving a 1.5 cm/scant ¾ inch overhang. Tuck this overhang under all around the rim so that the edge of the pastry case rises above the rim of the tin. Flute the edge. Fill the pastry case with the walnut and fig mixture and smooth the top.

Bake for 25 minutes. Remove from the oven and leave to cool to room temperature before serving, with a jug of cream or clotted cream.

BRUNO'S NOTES

This tart may also be served plain with tea or coffee in the afternoon, in which case it can be cut into 8 portions.

FRUITS POCHÉS, BISCUITS AU GINGEMBRE
Poached Fruits with Ginger Shortbread

SERVES 4

POACHED FRUITS
250 g/9 oz/1¼ cups sugar
1 vanilla pod (vanilla bean)
1 pear
1 small pineapple
4 damsons or other small tart plums
200 g/7 oz/about 1½ cups strawberries

GINGER SHORTBREAD
220 g/8 oz/2 sticks unsalted butter, at room temperature
100 g/3½ oz/½ cup caster sugar (U.S. granulated sugar)
185 g/6 oz/1¼ cups flour
100 g/3½ oz/¾ cup cornflour (cornstarch)
15 g/½ oz/2 tablespoons ground ginger
¼ teaspoon finely grated lemon zest

BRUNO'S NOTES

The ginger shortbread is best served slightly warm, so keep the dough in the refrigerator and bake just before eating.

I give this selection of fruits for poaching, but you can replace any of them as you wish.

FIRST poach the fruits. In a saucepan, combine 1 litre/1¾ pints/1 quart of water with the sugar. Split open the vanilla pod and add to the pan. Bring to the boil, stirring to dissolve the sugar, then reduce the heat so that the syrup is just simmering.

Peel the pear and cut it into quarters lengthways; cut out the core. Peel the pineapple, cut it into quarters lengthways and remove the core, then cut the pieces across into slices. Add the pear and pineapple to the syrup and simmer for 5 minutes.

Add the damsons and simmer for a further 2 minutes, then remove from the heat and put in the strawberries. Leave to cool completely, then place in the refrigerator to chill.

To make the ginger shortbread, put the soft butter and sugar in a food processor and mix until smooth. Add the flour, cornflour, ginger and lemon zest and process to form a ball of dough. Place the dough on a plate, cover and leave to rest in the refrigerator for 15 minutes.

Preheat the oven to 170°C/325°F/gas mark 3.

On a lightly floured surface, roll out the dough to 3–4 mm/about ⅛ inch thick and cut out squares or rounds or other shapes that you fancy. Place the shapes on a baking sheet lined with parchment paper.

Bake for about 20 minutes or until the shortbread is golden brown. Leave them to firm up on the baking sheet for a few minutes, then transfer them to a wire rack to cool.

Serve the poached fruits in soup plates, with the warm ginger shortbread.

TULES AUX ÉPICES
Spiced Almond and Coconut Biscuits

MAKES 25

100 g/3½ oz/1 cup flaked almonds (sliced almonds)
100 g/3½ oz/1 cup desiccated coconut (dried shredded coconut)
180 g/6 oz/¾ cup + 2 tablespoons caster sugar (U.S. granulated sugar)
30 g/1 oz/3 tablespoons flour
ground cinnamon
ground ginger
freshly grated nutmeg
3 egg whites (total weight 110 g/scant 4 oz)
40 g/1⅓ oz/2½ tablespoons unsalted butter, melted

I N a large bowl, combine the almonds, coconut, sugar, flour, 2 pinches of cinnamon, 4 pinches of ginger and 2 pinches of nutmeg. Add the egg whites and melted butter and mix together with a wooden spoon. Leave to rest in the refrigerator for 1 hour.

Preheat the oven to 160°C/325°F/gas mark 3.

Line several baking sheets with parchment paper. Drop teaspoonfuls of the mixture on to the paper, spacing them well apart to allow for spreading. Make them as flat as possible using a fork dipped in milk. Bake for 6–8 minutes or until a nice golden brown.

Using a slotted spatula, lift the biscuits, one by one, from the baking sheet and lay them quickly over a bottle or a rolling pin to give them the traditional roof-tile shape. Leave to cool and set on the bottle or rolling pin.

BRUNO'S NOTES

These biscuits are best baked in batches so that you can shape and cool one batch while the next one is in the oven. If you are interrupted while lifting the biscuits from the baking sheet, they may cool and become too firm to shape, but you can put them back into the oven for a few moments to soften them again.

Serve these with creamy desserts and with ice creams and sorbets. You can also shape the biscuits into cups by laying them over an orange or an upturned glass, and then fill them with a fruit salad.

CRÈME RENVERSÉE AU CARAMEL
Upside-Down Caramel Cream

SERVES 4

100 g/3½ oz Genoese or other sponge cake
a demitasse cup of very strong black coffee
100 g/3½ oz/½ cup caster sugar
½ vanilla pod (vanilla bean)
500 ml/16 fl oz milk
4 eggs

P REHEAT the oven to 190°C/375°F/gas mark 5.

Slice the sponge cake and lay the slices over the bottoms of four 9 cm/ 3½ inch diameter soufflé dishes, each 4.5 cm/scant 5 inches deep. Pour over the coffee and leave to soak.

BRUNO'S NOTES

When you add the boiling water to the caramel, cover your hand with an oven glove or towel because the very hot caramel is likely to spit.

Melt half of the sugar in a small saucepan and cook until it turns to a hazelnut-coloured caramel. Remove from the heat and dip the base of the pan in cold water to stop the caramel cooking. Add 1 tablespoon of boiling water to the caramel and stir to mix, then pour immediately over the sponge cake.

Split the vanilla pod open lengthways and put it in a heavy-based saucepan with the milk. Bring to the boil.

Meanwhile, mix the eggs with the remaining sugar in a bowl. Pour the boiling milk into the egg mixture, stirring well, then strain through a fine sieve into the soufflé dishes. Place the soufflé dishes in a roasting tin and pour enough hot water into the tin to come halfway up the sides of the dishes. Cook in the oven for 30 minutes or until the custard is just set.

Remove the soufflé dishes from the *bain-marie* of hot water and leave to cool completely.

To serve, turn out upside-down on to serving dishes.

SALADE DE FRUITS ÉXOTIQUES À L'ANIS ET EAU DE ROSE
Salad of Exotic Fruits Flavoured with Star Anise and Rosewater

SERVES 4

a selection of exotic fruits such as mango, papaya, passion fruit, prickly pear, guava, pineapple, kiwi fruit, grapefruit and so on
2 tablespoons rosewater

SYRUP
100 g/3½ oz/½ cup sugar
pared zest of 1 lemon
2 star anise
5 green peppercorns
a small bunch of fresh mint

BRUNO'S NOTES

Star anise should be available in a large supermarket, and in Chinese and Indian shops. Rosewater can also be found in Indian shops.

TO make the syrup, put the sugar in a saucepan with 150 ml/5 fl oz of water and add the lemon zest. Bring to the boil, stirring to dissolve the sugar. Add the star anise and lightly crushed peppercorns and boil for 2 minutes. Roughly chop the mint and stir into the syrup. Remove from the heat, cover and leave to infuse and cool.

Meanwhile, peel and stone the fruits if necessary. Cut the fruits into different shapes – balls, cubes, slices and so on – and put into a bowl.

Strain the cold syrup over the fruits and put into the refrigerator to chill for at least 2 hours.

Illustrated on PLATE 32

Just before serving, stir in the rosewater.

FIGUES CONFITES À L'ANIS, PARFAIT À LA VERVEINE

Poached Fresh Figs with Star Anise, Strega Parfait

SERVES 4

8 fresh figs
225 g/8 oz/1 cup + 2 tablespoons sugar
1 teaspoon fennel seeds
1 star anise
¼ cinnamon stick

PARFAIT
3 egg yolks
30 g/1 oz/2½ tablespoons sugar
2 tablespoons Strega liqueur or Verveine du Velay liqueur
150 ml/5 fl oz whipping cream

BRUNO'S NOTES

The components of this dessert can be prepared the day before and then dressed on the plate just before serving.

FIRST make the parfait. In a large heatproof bowl placed over a pan of simmering water, whisk the egg yolks with 2 tablespoons of hot water until five times the original volume. Remove the bowl from the hot water and set aside.

In a medium-sized saucepan, combine the sugar and 3½ tablespoons of cold water. Bring to the boil, stirring to dissolve the sugar. Boil for 2 minutes. Pour the syrup in a thin stream over the egg yolk mixture, whisking constantly, and continue whisking until cold. Add the liqueur to this *sabayon*.

In another large bowl, whip the cream until thick but not stiff. Pour the *sabayon* over the cream and fold together quickly with a large spoon.

Place four 5 cm/2 inch flan rings or muffin rings on a baking tray and fill each with the parfait mixture. Smooth the tops level. Cover and freeze for 6 hours.

While the parfait is freezing, prepare the figs. Rinse the figs very well under cold running water, then put them in a saucepan and cover with 500 ml/16 fl oz of hot water. Add the sugar, fennel seeds, star anise and cinnamon stick. Bring to a simmer, stirring occasionally to dissolve the sugar, then leave to cook gently for 30 minutes.

Remove the figs with a slotted spoon and set aside. Reduce the syrup by half. Strain the syrup into a bowl; return the star anise to the syrup and crumble in the cinnamon. Put the figs back into the syrup and leave to cool completely. When cold, put into the refrigerator to chill.

To serve, unmould the parfait rounds into soup plates and place the figs on top. Spoon over the syrup and serve immediately.

COUPE GIVRÉE MOKA
Iced Mocha Cup

SERVES 4

GRANITÉ
100 g/3½ oz/½ cup sugar
5 tablespoons instant coffee powder

CHOCOLATE MOUSSE
100 g/3½ oz best-quality bittersweet chocolate
20 g/⅔ oz/1½ tablespoons unsalted butter
3 tablespoons caster sugar (superfine sugar)
3 eggs, separated
salt

CHICORY CREAM
200 ml/7 fl oz whipping cream
chicory essence, or dark treacle or molasses
unsweetened cocoa powder

BRUNO'S NOTES

Once the granité is ready, it can be kept in the freezer up to 3 hours, so you can make it in the afternoon for dinner.

To make the granité, put the sugar and 400 ml/14 fl oz of water in a saucepan and bring to the boil, stirring occasionally to dissolve the sugar. Stir in the coffee powder, then remove from the heat and allow to cool.

Pour the cold liquid into a baking tin and put into the freezer. When 1 cm/½ inch all around the edge of the granité has set, stir this frozen mixture into the liquid in the centre. Return to the freezer, and stir again when the edge has set. Continue in this way, to obtain flakes of frozen granité.

While the granité is freezing, make the chocolate mousse. Put the chocolate and butter in a heatproof bowl and set it in a pan of hot water. Stir until the mixture is melted and smooth. Add 1 tablespoon of the sugar and stir until it has dissolved, then remove the bowl from the *bain-marie* of hot water. Incorporate the egg yolks, one by one.

Whisk the egg whites with a tiny pinch of salt until stiff, then whisk in the remaining sugar. Fold the egg whites gently but thoroughly into the chocolate mixture using a large spoon. Put into the refrigerator to set.

Whip the cream with the chicory essence or treacle or molasses until stiff but not buttery. Keep in the refrigerator until you are ready to assemble the dessert.

To serve, into each of 4 glass coupes, put one-quarter of the chocolate mousse, then one-quarter of the granité, and finally one-quarter of the chicory cream. Sprinkle the tops with a little cocoa powder through a sieve, and serve immediately.

PÊCHES LAQUÉES AUX ÉPICES
Peaches Glazed with Spices

SERVES 4

½ teaspoon coriander seeds
½ teaspoon Szechuan pepper
⅓ stick of cinnamon
grated zest of ½ lemon
60 g/2 oz/½ cup blanched almonds
200 g/7 oz/1 cup sugar
4 large peaches
30 g/1 oz/2 tablespoons unsalted butter
5 tablespoons acacia honey
fresh mint leaves, to decorate

ON a chopping board, with the bottom of a very heavy pan, crush the spices very finely. If necessary, finish with a knife. Add the lemon zest and the coarsely chopped almonds and put aside.

Combine 1 litre/1¾ pints/1 quart of water with the sugar in a large saucepan and bring to the boil, stirring to dissolve the sugar. Put the peaches into this syrup and simmer for 2 minutes, then remove from the heat and set aside to cool. When the peaches are cool enough to handle, peel them and put them back into the syrup.

About 10 minutes before serving, melt the butter in another pan and stir in the honey and the spice mixture. Toss the drained peaches in the mixture until they are glazed (about 5 minutes.)

Spoon the peaches on to plates, sprinkle over some mint leaves, and serve with a sorbet or ice cream of your choice.

BRUNO'S NOTES

The syrup used for poaching the peaches can be kept and employed again for poaching fruit. Or add a little rosewater to taste and 1 teaspoon of egg white, and freeze in an electric ice cream machine until softly set to make a sorbet.

SALADE DE FRUITS ROUGES, GLACE AU KÜMMEL
Salad of Red Fruits with Kümmel Sorbet

SERVES 4

60 g/2 oz/5 tablespoons sugar
12 green peppercorns
a strip of orange zest
200 g/7 oz/1½ cups raspberries
150 g/5 oz/1¼ cups redcurrants
150 g/5 oz/about 1 cup strawberries
sprigs of fresh mint to decorate

BRUNO'S NOTES

If you prefer, you can make a kümmel granité rather than the sorbet. Leave out the egg white, and follow the instructions for making the granité for Coupe Givrée Moka (page 143).

SORBET
100 g/3½ oz/½ cup sugar
1 teaspoon caraway seeds
¼ egg white
1½ tablespoons kümmel

PUT the sugar in a small saucepan with 100 ml/3½ fl oz of water. Slightly crush the green peppercorns with the side of a knife and add to the pan with the orange zest. Bring to the boil, stirring to dissolve the sugar. Remove from the heat and allow to cool completely.

Combine the raspberries, redcurrants and strawberries in a bowl. Pour over the cold syrup and turn the fruits gently to mix. Leave in the refrigerator to macerate for at least 2 hours.

To make the sorbet, put the sugar and caraway seeds in a saucepan and add 200 ml/7 fl oz of water. Bring to the boil, stirring to dissolve the sugar. Strain the syrup through a fine sieve into a cold bowl. When completely cold, stir in the egg white and kümmel. Pour into an electric ice cream machine and churn for about 15 minutes or until softly set.

To serve, divide the fruits and their syrup among soup plates or dessert bowls. Add a scoop of kümmel sorbet and a sprig of fresh mint to each.

GELÉE DE FRAMBOISES ET SORBET DE MELON CHARENTAIS
Fresh Raspberry Jelly and Melon Sorbet

SERVES 4

1 leaf of gelatine
80 g/2¾ oz/6½ tablespoons sugar with pectin
500 g/1 lb 2 oz/2 pints raspberries
1 ripe melon, preferably a charentais or cavaillon with orange flesh
juice of ½ lime
¼ egg white
leaves of fresh mint, to decorate

SOAK the gelatine leaf in cold water to soften it.
Meanwhile, combine the sugar and 300 ml/10 fl oz of water in a saucepan and bring to the boil, stirring occasionally to dissolve the sugar. Remove from the heat and put the raspberries into this syrup. Squeeze the gelatine leaf and add to the raspberry mixture. Stir until the gelatine has dissolved. Divide the jelly among 4 soup plates. Place in the refrigerator to set.

Peel the melon, and remove and discard the seeds. Liquidise the flesh with the lime juice until smooth. Press the melon *coulis* through a fine sieve to remove any fibres, then pour into an electric ice cream machine and add the egg white. Churn for about 15 minutes or until softly set.

To serve, top each serving of raspberry jelly with 3 *quenelles* of melon sorbet, and garnish with mint leaves.

Illustrated on PLATE 28

Champignons à l'huile infusée

Légumes au vinaigre

'Chutney' de fruits secs

Tomates douces sechées au 'soleil'

Concombres à l'aigre doux

Fruits pochés au sirop

Kumkats aigre-doux

Vin aux figues

Vin de noix

Vin aux agrumes

Vin de framboises

Hydromel

Cerises à la grappa

CHAPTER SEVEN

Les Conserves

PRESERVES

Preserving is a useful technique which changes the flavour and textures of certain ingredients, enabling them to be kept for a period of time. The best ingredients for preserving are those usually difficult to find or, rather, to find of good enough quality. Many of the preserves here are used quite often in my cooking.

CHAMPIGNONS À L'HUILE INFUSÉE
Mushrooms Preserved in Oil

100 g/3½ oz fresh girolles
200 g/7 oz white button mushrooms
100 ml/3½ fl oz white wine vinegar
1 teaspoon salt
3 cloves of garlic
1 bay leaf
a bunch of fresh thyme
10 black peppercorns
olive oil

TRIM and clean all the mushrooms.
In a non-reactive saucepan, combine the vinegar, salt, the garlic slightly crushed with the side of a knife, the bay leaf, thyme, peppercorns and 200 ml/7 fl oz of water. Bring to the boil.

Add the mushrooms and blanch for 30 seconds, then drain the mushrooms and flavourings in a sieve.

Pack the mushrooms and flavourings into a clean jar and cover with olive oil. Seal and keep in a cool place.

BRUNO'S NOTES

I like these mushrooms with apéritifs or in a green salad with some croûtons. The vinegar used for blanching the mushrooms can be kept and used in salad dressings.

LÉGUMES AU VINAIGRE
Pickled Vegetables

250 g/9 oz carrots
200 g/7 oz cucumber
200 g/7 oz pickling onions
250 g/9 oz cauliflower

MARINADE
300 ml/10 fl oz white wine vinegar
1 teaspoon coriander seeds
10 black peppercorns
3 cloves of garlic
1 bay leaf
4 tablespoons clear honey
1 teaspoon mustard seed (optional)
1 teaspoon salt

PEEL the carrots and cut them across into sections 3 cm/1¼ inches long. Cut these pieces lengthways into 5 mm/¼ inch thick sticks.

BRUNO'S NOTES

Serve these pickled vegetables with pâtés, charcuterie and cold meats.

Peel the cucumber, cut it in half lengthways and remove the seeds. Then cut it into sticks the same size as the carrots.

Peel the onions. Cut the cauliflower into little florets.

In a non-reactive saucepan, combine all the ingredients for the marinade with 200 ml/7 fl oz of water. Bring to the boil and boil for 30 seconds. Add the onions and 30 seconds later add the carrots and cauliflower. Remove from the heat and leave to cool until completely cold. Then add the cucumber.

Pour the vegetables and marinade into a glass jar or bowl and cover. Leave to marinate for at least 48 hours before serving.

'CHUTNEY' DE FRUITS SECS
Dried Fruit Chutney

100 g/3½ oz dates
100 g/3½ oz prunes
100 g/3½ oz dried apricots
100 g/3½ oz dried figs
100 g/3½ oz sultanas (golden raisins)
100 g/3½ oz onions
5 cm/2 inch piece of fresh root ginger
100 g/3½ oz/7 tablespoons unsalted butter
3 cloves of garlic
5 leaves of fresh sage (optional)
1 teaspoon quatre-épices
3 tablespoons tomato paste
1 green apple
200 ml/7 fl oz malt vinegar
5 tablespoons HP Sauce
1 teaspoon salt

BRUNO'S NOTES

I love this chutney. Its sweet and sour-spicy flavour goes very well with meat pâtés. I always have a pot in my refrigerator at home.

Quatre-épices is a blend of four spices, usually cloves, ginger, pepper and nutmeg. If you cannot find it in the shops, you can substitute mixed spice.

TAKE the stones out of the dates and prunes. Put all the dried fruits in a saucepan, cover with cold water and bring to the boil. Boil for 5 minutes, then remove from the heat and set aside to soak for 1 hour. This operation will soften the fruits and extract some of the sugar.

Peel and finely chop the onions and ginger. In a large, heavy saucepan, melt the butter and cook the onions for 4–5 minutes. Add the finely chopped garlic, chopped sage leaves, ginger, *quatre-épices* and, last, the tomato paste. Stir well and leave to cook on a low heat for 5 minutes.

Meanwhile, drain the dried fruits and chop them with a knife or in the food processor for 1 minute. Peel, core and dice the apple. Add the dried fruits and apple to the onion mixture with the vinegar, HP Sauce, salt and 200 ml/7 fl oz of water. Cook very gently for 1 hour, stirring occasionally.

Leave the chutney to cool, then ladle it into jars. Cover and store in the refrigerator, where it will keep for up to 3 weeks.

TOMATES DOUCES SECHÉES AU 'SOLEIL'

'Sun-Dried' Tomatoes

2 kg/4½ lb ripe plum-type or large Italian tomatoes
salt
2 star anise
a bunch of fresh rosemary
5 cloves of garlic
1 bay leaf
virgin olive oil

PREHEAT the oven to 140°C/275°F/gas mark 1.
Cut the tomatoes in half lengthways. With a spoon, remove and discard the seeds. Sprinkle the inside of each tomato half with salt.

Put a wire rack in a baking tray and arrange the tomatoes, cut sides down, on the rack. Put them in the oven to dry for about 12 hours.

Remove the tomatoes from the oven and set aside to cool.

Drop the star anise into a small pan of boiling water and boil for 30 seconds. Drain.

In a large sterilised jar, arrange the tomatoes with the rosemary, peeled cloves of garlic, star anise and bay leaf. Pour in enough olive oil to cover. Close the jar and store in a cool, dark place for 2 weeks before using.

BRUNO'S NOTES

Of course, the original way of drying tomatoes is to put them in the sunshine, but British weather being what it is, I suggest this method instead.

It is important that the tomatoes be dried enough so that they don't give out any water if you squeeze them, but don't leave them in the oven until they become crispy.

CONCOMBRES À L'AIGRE DOUX

Pickled Cucumbers

2 cucumbers
2 tablespoons salt
200 ml/7 fl oz white wine vinegar
2 tablespoons honey
1 clove of garlic
1 teaspoon green peppercorns
20 coriander seeds
a bunch of fresh thyme
a bunch of fresh dill

PEEL the cucumbers and cut them across into 3 cm/1¼ inch sections.
Trim the sections to square the sides, then cut into 1 cm/½ inch thick

sticks. Don't keep any sticks that are just made up of seeds. Alternatively, cut the peeled cucumbers in half lengthways, remove the seeds and then cut crossways into 1 cm/$\frac{1}{2}$ inch wide half-moons.

Put the cucumber sticks in a bowl and sprinkle over 1 tablespoon of salt. Set aside for 10 minutes.

Meanwhile, combine the vinegar, honey, garlic crushed with the side of a knife, the peppercorns, coriander seeds, herbs and remaining salt in a saucepan. Bring to the boil, then remove from the heat and leave to cool completely.

Rinse the cucumber sticks under cold running water and pat dry with paper towels. Put the cucumber into a clean jar or glass bowl and pour over the cold vinegar mixture.

Cover tightly and put into the refrigerator. Leave for 2 days before using, and store in the refrigerator.

FRUITS POCHÉS AU SIROP
Poached Fruits in Syrup

fresh, ripe pears, peaches, apricots, cherries or plums
450 g/1 lb/2$\frac{1}{4}$ cups sugar
1 vanilla pod (vanilla bean)
juice of $\frac{1}{2}$ lemon

BRUNO'S NOTES

In winter, these fruits will be very welcome in fruit salads, as a filling for tarts, in a pavlova or in other desserts.

THE fruits used must be in perfect condition – clean and not over-ripe. Wash them in cold water, then drain in a colander, always handling with great care.

Peel and core pears, and dip them in lemon water to prevent discoloration. Blanch apricots, plums and peaches in boiling water for 1 minute, then peel, cut in half and remove the stones.

Dissolve the sugar in 1.2 litres/2 pints/5 cups of water with the vanilla pod and lemon juice. Bring slowly to the boil and boil for 1 minute. Remove from the heat and cool completely.

Pack the fruits into sterilised jars with the help of a wooden spoon. Pour in enough cold syrup to come to the top of the fruits. Tap the jar with your hands to make sure the syrup goes everywhere in the jar and that there are no air pockets. Secure the jars with spring clip and rubber band or screw-band.

Place the jars in a very large and deep pan, making sure they do not touch each other. Cover with cold water, put a lid on the pan and bring slowly to the boil. Boil gently for 15 minutes (or 30 minutes for pears). The temperature of the water should be maintained at 83°C/182°F (88°C/190°F for pears).

Lift the jars out of the water and leave them for 24 hours before testing that the seal has worked. Store in a cool, dark place.

KUMKATS AIGRE-DOUX
Pickled Kumquats

500 g/1 lb 2 oz kumquats
1 teaspoon salt
200 ml/7 fl oz white wine vinegar
1 clove
3 cardamom pods
4 tablespoons clear honey

BRUNO'S NOTES

Serve this pickle with a duck or game terrine, or add a spoonful to the gravy for a roast duck.

CUT all the kumquats in half, then put them in a saucepan. Cover with cold water, add the salt and bring to the boil. Simmer for 5 minutes. Drain the fruits and allow them to cool, then chop roughly on a board.

Put the vinegar, clove, crushed cardamom pods and honey in a non-reactive saucepan and bring to the boil. Add the kumquats. Ladle the mixture into a sterilised jar, cover tightly and store in the refrigerator for 1 month before serving.

VIN AUX FIGUES
Fig Wine

500 g/1 lb 2 oz dried figs
1 bay leaf
½ orange
1 tablespoon coriander seeds
1 stick of cinnamon
2 cardamom pods
200 ml/7 fl oz Madeira
2 litres/3½ pints/2 quarts red wine
100 ml/3½ fl oz brandy

BRUNO'S NOTES

This is a wine for cooking, not drinking. It is delicious in sauces for game and red meat or in confits. To use, strain the wine; cut the figs into small cubes and add to the finished sauce.

PLACE the figs in a large saucepan and cover with cold water. Bring slowly to the boil and simmer for 5 minutes, then drain and rinse with cold water.

Return the figs to the pan and add the bay leaf, sliced orange, coriander seeds, cinnamon stick, lightly crushed cardamom pods, Madeira and red wine. Bring to the boil and simmer for 10 minutes. Remove from the heat and leave to cool completely.

Add the brandy, then pour the fig wine into jars and seal tightly. Leave for 1 month before using.

VIN DE NOIX
Walnut Wine

20 young and very green walnuts
500 g/1 lb 2 oz/2½ cups sugar
1.5 litres/2½ pints/1½ quarts red wine
500 ml/16 fl oz brandy

BRUNO'S NOTES

You don't need to use a good quality red wine to make this.

The walnut wine can be served as an apéritif, or used in both sweet and savoury dishes, particularly for game.

In France, we have an adage that says to make a superb walnut wine, you need to pick the walnuts on the night of 29 June.

WITH a heavy knife, cut the walnuts into pieces and put them in a bowl. Add the sugar, wine and brandy and mix well. Pour into a sterilised jar, cover tightly and leave to macerate for 1 month.

Strain the wine through a sieve and then through muslin or cheesecloth. Pour it into sterilised bottles, seal with new corks and leave for 2 months before serving.

VIN AUX AGRUMES
Citrus Fruit Wine

MAKES 8 litres/14 pints/2 gallons

5 ripe oranges
4 limes
1 grapefruit
1.5 kg/3¼ lb/7½ cups sugar
5 litres/8 pints/5 quarts dry white wine, such as a Chardonnay
1.5 litres/2½ pints/1½ quarts grappa
1 vanilla pod (vanilla bean)
1 cinnamon stick
10 cardamom pods

BRUNO'S NOTES

Serve this wine with desserts, or on hot days mixed with lemonade and fresh mint like Pimm's.

Of course, you can make the wine in smaller quantities, but you'll find it goes fast.

SCRUB the fruits thoroughly and rinse well, then slice them and place in a large sterilised bowl. Mix together the sugar, wine, grappa, vanilla pod, cinnamon stick, and lightly crushed cardamom pods and pour over the fruit. Cover and leave in a cool place for 72 hours, stirring with a wooden spoon every 12 hours.

Ladle the fruit and liquid into sterilised glass preserving jars and store in a cool place for 2 months.

Strain the wine through a nylon jelly bag or a muslin- or cheesecloth-lined funnel into sterilised bottles. Boil the corks in water for 5 minutes, then use to seal the bottles. Store in a cool place.

VIN DE FRAMBOISES
Raspberry Wine

1.3 kg/2¾ lb/about 5 pints raspberries
2 litres/3½ pints/2 quarts red wine, preferably burgundy
400 g/14 oz/2 cups sugar
1 vanilla pod (vanilla bean)
300 ml/10 fl oz brandy

L IQUIDISE the raspberries to make a purée, then rub the purée through a nylon sieve to remove the seeds. You should have about 1 litre/1¾ pints/1 quart of raspberry purée.

In a large saucepan, combine the raspberry purée, wine, sugar and vanilla pod split open. Bring to the boil and boil for 30 seconds, skimming off all the scum that forms on the surface. Remove the pan from the heat, put on a lid and leave to cool completely.

Strain the liquid through muslin or cheesecloth into a bowl. Stir in the brandy. Pour this wine into sterilised bottles, seal with new corks and store in a cool place for at least 1 month before serving.

BRUNO'S NOTES
This is a wonderful dessert wine. Once opened, store it in the refrigerator.

HYDROMEL
Honey-Flavoured Wine

MAKES 2.5 litres/4 pints/2½ quarts

2 tablespoons coriander seeds
250 g/9 oz/¾ cup liquid honey
a large strip of orange zest
250 ml/8 fl oz brandy
2 litres/3½ pints/2 quarts Sauternes wine

I N a small pan, heat the coriander seeds for about 2 minutes or until you smell the strong coriander flavour.

Tip the seeds into a large bowl and add all the other ingredients. Mix well, then put into sterilised jars. Cover tightly. Set aside in a cool place to steep for 2 weeks.

Strain through a nylon jelly bag, or muslin or cheesecloth, and pour into sterilised bottles. Close each with a new cork. Store in a cool place.

BRUNO'S NOTES
I use acacia honey to make this wine. My brother, Christian, who lives in Libourne, keeps bees as a hobby – he has 30 hives – and so we are always well supplied with wonderful honey.

I like to use Hydromel in game sauces – it is a particularly good complement to a roast duck or pigeon. Add a good quantity of Hydromel when deglazing the roasting tin, then reduce with stock to make a rich sauce. Hydromel will keep quite a long time, although I've never been able to test just how long as it gets used up quickly in my kitchen.

CERISES À LA GRAPPA
Cherries in Grappa

200 g/7 oz/1 cup sugar
2 strips of orange zest
500 g/1 lb 2 oz/about 2 pints fresh cherries
1 litre/1¾ pints/1 quart grappa

BRUNO'S NOTES

Serve this liqueur, with the cherries, in a small liqueur glass to drink with your after-dinner coffee.

PUT the sugar and orange zest in a saucepan with 200 ml/7 fl oz of water. Bring to the boil, stirring to dissolve the sugar, then remove from the heat and leave to cool.

Meanwhile, wash the cherries well and dry them completely with paper towels. With scissors, trim the stalks to half their length.

Put the cherries into sterilised jars. Stir the grappa into the syrup, then pour it over the cherries to cover them. Close the jars tightly and store in a cool, dark place for at least 1 month before serving.

INDEX

ACKNOWLEDGEMENTS

These are the people who have given me their support, which is always much needed in following such a hard profession. I would like to say thank you very much to my dear wife Catherine; to Alastair Little, for his support from my early beginnings in England; to Annabel Wyatt, who organised the making of this book; to Ramon Pajares and the Inn on the Park Hotel, without whom this book would not have been possible, and to Norma MacMillan for her patience and invaluable help in the writing.